Learning from
Case Studies

Learning from Case Studies

GEOFF EASTON
University of Lancaster

Prentice/Hall International

Englewood Cliffs, New Jersey · London · New Delhi
Sydney · Toronto · Tokyo · Singapore · Wellington

British Library Cataloguing in Publication Data

Easton, Geoff
  Learning from case studies.
  1. Management—Study and Teaching—Great Britain
  2. Case method
  I. Title
  658'.007'1   HF1142.G7

  ISBN 0-13-527416-8

ISBN 0-13-527416-8

PRENTICE-HALL INTERNATIONAL, INC., *London*
PRENTICE-HALL OF AUSTRALIA PTY. LTD., *Sydney*
PRENTICE-HALL OF CANADA, INC., *Toronto*
PRENTICE-HALL OF INDIA PRIVATE LTD., *New Delhi*
PRENTICE-HALL OF JAPAN, INC., *Tokyo*
PRENTICE-HALL OF SOUTHEAST ASIA PTE., LTD., *Singapore*
PRENTICE-HALL, INC., *Englewood Cliffs, New Jersey*
WHITEHALL BOOKS LIMITED, *Wellington, New Zealand*

Printed in Great Britain by A. Wheaton & Co., Ltd., Exeter

10 9 8 7 6

To

Helen

George

Jonathan

Contents

Preface

One trend in education in the 1970s is likely to continue with increasing vigour in the 1980s. Students have begun to demand relevance in courses that claim to be in any way applied or vocational. This is particularly true of the applied social sciences such as management, social administration, education, architecture and environmental planning. Continuing high rates of unemployment and uncertainties about an energy-deficient world economy have sobered a whole generation of students. Many now demand to be made as marketable as possible.

They are therefore very receptive to methods of learning which allow them a glimpse of the world they will be entering. These methods attempt to simulate reality in the classroom. They include projects, exercises, games, role playing and, of course, case studies.

The introduction of these new learning methods has not been wholly successful. A number of major hurdles stand in the way. In particular the case method has suffered from a student backlash. This can be attributed to a number of factors. Simulation learning methods are prodigal of resources, difficult to schedule, organize and control, and raise many assessment problems. In short, they do not integrate well with existing teaching methods. Of these methods, however, the case study is the least radical. It has therefore been a favourite addition to existing courses. 'Let's give them a case or two—that should keep them happy', has too often been the response to students' demands for relevance. This has sometimes resulted in excessive and inappropriate use of the case method.

Another factor affecting the use, and abuse, of case studies is lack of teacher training. Few UK case leaders have had any formal instruction in the case method. Most have learned to lead cases by being thrown in at the deep end. This leads too many of them to believe that their students should receive the same treatment. It is even possible to rationalize this approach:

'Students must be given room to explore.'
'Students mustn't become too dependent on teachers.'
'They're always wanting to know the "right" answer; the case method has no right answer. It's my job to keep them confused.'

All of these comments may be valid in particular circumstances. Too frequently they hide a basic problem. Case instructors know how they analyse cases but cannot, or will not, pass this knowledge on to their students.

Cases involve a lot of hard work for students. They often stimulate students to efforts far beyond those devoted to more conventional learning methods. Unfortunately much of this effort is wasted. If this were true only of the first few cases in a case course, then there would be no problem, but it is frequently true that students are no nearer understanding what cases are all about at the end of the course than they were at the beginning. Is it any wonder that they become frustrated, bored, unhappy and finally disenchanted with the case method? Add to this the need to pass a case examination, and the current ground-swell of opinion against the use of cases can be understood.

Yet these problems can be solved. No teacher would wish to prevent a student from exploring, but he should not ask him to do so without the necessary equipment. Thrust back on their own resources most students learn some of the necessary skills, but do so rather inefficiently; some students learn no skills at all. Put another way, the gap between conventional and simulation learning methods is too great. Conventional learning methods require students to accept and learn the concepts, principles and techniques that the teacher thinks will be useful. Simulation learning methods ask students to invent their own concepts, principles and techniques. This gap can and should be bridged.

This book sprang out of an increasing awareness that case studies, as they are normally used, are inefficient teaching vehicles. Beginning case analysts require guidelines to help them negotiate the first few obstacles to learning. These guidelines are not intended to be, and indeed they could not be, a complete guide to action. They are a base from which to develop a personal approach.

I have tried to test these guidelines on case courses I have taught, and invariably they have resulted in much improved case performances. Discussions have been more sharply focused and the gap between the expertise of the case leader and the students has been narrowed. Yet this has not stunted creativity: rather, creativity has been stimulated towards more specific ends.

Case analysis is meant to provide practice in problem solving and decision-making in a simulated situation. The guidelines were therefore developed from some of the current principles and theories of problem solving and decision-making. These have been interpreted and simplified in order to create a set of practical rules which could be followed in one specific situation—the case analysis. This book therefore goes beyond what is normally found in a student guide to case analysis: it may even make a modest contribution to the field by integrating a number of different approaches. The main criterion in writing this book was always, 'Will it work in a case analysis situation?'. I hope to demonstrate that it will work by using specific cases to illustrate how the guidelines may be used.

This book is aimed at students at a number of different levels. A step by step approach is described. Within each step a number of more sophisticated and therefore more effective techniques are discussed. The beginner may feel that he can only cope with the most basic steps: a more experienced case analyst could proceed much further and employ many more techniques. The choice is left to the individual; it is a question of balancing time and effort against the rewards of acquiring more skills.

A number of people have helped me in the twin tasks of clarifying my ideas on the case method and of putting those ideas on paper. My major debt is to Professor Ken Simmonds of the London Business School. He was my first case instructor and, in the light of experience, the best. It was a powerful combination and the impetus it gave to my interest in the case method has kept me enthusiastic ever since. George Long and Jackie Marrian, present and past directors of the MA in Marketing Education at Lancaster, have contributed a great deal to my understanding of management learning experiences. Our discussions have always been interesting, usually enjoyable and sometimes hilarious. Past MA in Marketing Education students must also be thanked for the part they have played as guinea pigs, sounding boards and leg-men.

Much of this book was written in Honolulu at the University of Hawaii on an exchange visit I made there in 1979/80. I would like to thank Ed Faison and Laurie Jacobs of the University of Hawaii, and Peter Spillard of the University of Lancaster, for making the impossible possible. Gladys Kuwata typed most of the first draft and thanks are due to her as well as to Lesley Kyle, Judith Feltham and June Johnson who continued the (almost) thankless task of deciphering my increasingly indecipherable writing.

Finally my wife, Helen, and sons, Jonathan and George, by heroically resisting the temptation to invade my study, helped me to complete the book sooner than I had a right to expect.

Geoff Easton

Learning from
Case Studies

CHAPTER 1

The Case Method

1.1 THE CASE

A case, short for case history, is a description of a situation. The typical case consists of a few pages of written description of an actual situation facing an organization. It will usually describe how the current position developed and what problem a key personality in the case is currently facing. Tables of data, diagrams and photographs may be necessary to help provide a complete picture. Appendices are normally used to include large amounts of data that would otherwise clutter the text.

There are many variations on this basic theme. Cases may be a few sentences or hundreds of pages long. Students taking their first case course usually associate length with difficulty. This is a dangerous principle: many short cases prove to be very taxing. All of the insignificant detail has been stripped away and the student has to tackle basic issues head on. By contrast, some long cases generate little conflict since there seem to be so few alternatives to choose from. It is never wise to judge a case by its length.

Cases are normally written but there is no reason why this should be the sole form of communication. Film, video and audio tapes and tape/slide sequences have all been used as vehicles for case descriptions. These all serve to make the case more realistic for the student. However, they also create problems. Written information is easier to work with and analyse than the information contained in, for example, a film. It becomes necessary to summarize the information from the film in written form. This is not only time-consuming but can also lead to all sorts of errors. Multi-media cases are for students who have already mastered the written case.

Although cases normally involve organizations, they need not do so. Cases describing the problems of individuals, couples, groups, social institutions or even nations may be used in particular educational situations. Cases are not confined to use by business or management students. They are used in social administration, psychiatry, architectural studies,

1

education, engineering and have potential in any discipline where the
skills of solving complex unstructured problems are required. After all the
case method has its origins in the methods used to teach Harvard lawyers.
In this book the examples used will be largely from business. However,
the basic principles put forward are general enough to apply to any situation where the case method is used.

Cases may be accurate descriptions of real situations or they may be
works of fiction. Most cases fall somewhere between these two extremes.
Organizations frequently require that their identities be disguised for
fear of revealing information which might be of use to competitors. This
may simply mean a fictitious name is used. In other cases many of the
data fundamental to an understanding of a case are changed. This can
have unfortunate results. One technique is simply to multiply all the
figures by a constant factor such as 3.4. This maintains the relationship
within the particular set of data. However, it distorts the relationship
between this set of data and the data in the rest of the case. For example,
inflating profit and loss account figures may suggest that a company has
the resources to do things which in reality it would not be capable of
doing. Casewriters may also 'rewrite history' to suit a specific educational
objective.

A case is *not* the truth, the whole truth and nothing but the truth. For
reasons mentioned above it may be partly a work of fiction. In any case it
is necessarily a partial and incomplete description. It should therefore be
approached in a questioning rather than an accepting frame of mind.
Students too often treat the information in a case as gospel. In chapter 3
we shall look at the kinds of information a case contains and try to assess
how valid the information in a case is.

Some cases are entirely fictitious. This may occur when access to real
life situations is restricted or where the casewriter wishes to explore a
particular problem. In these instances you are relying on the literary
talents and experience of the casewriter to produce a self-consistent and
believable situation. Many students do not like fictitious cases. They do
not get the profound sense of involvement that comes with knowing they
are examining the workings of a real situation. Nevertheless, they can be
very important and useful when the alternative is having no satisfactory
case at all which fits the bill.

1.2 WAYS IN WHICH CASES ARE USED

The case method in most people's minds is the method used to teach
MBA students at Harvard Business School. In reality of course there are
a vast range of alternative ways in which cases can be used.

It is useful first of all to distinguish between cases and exercises. An exercise may superficially resemble a case in that it is also a description of an actual or fictitious situation. However, the objectives of using an exercise are different. An exercise provides the material for a student to learn to apply a particular concept, technique or principle. A case is used to help students learn a broad range of skills. An exercise has a solution and one way of reaching that solution. A case has many solutions and many alternative pathways to reach them.

Again there is a middle ground. Many cases are written to allow students to practise particular analytical techniques or to approach problems in a particular way. Students may even be directed to use certain techniques or given specific questions to answer. While this gives them some of the flavour of an exercise, they still remain cases. The central function of the case method is to teach students to solve complex unstructured problems. There is no analytical technique or approach which can solve these kinds of problems. Some can help, but in the case method their use will always be subsidiary to the central purpose of using cases as a learning method. If a student is confused about whether a case is being used as a case or as an exercise, it is well worth discussing the problem with the instructor involved. It is always possible that the instructor has not clearly made the distinction in his own mind.

Cases can also be 'dead' or 'live' or somewhere in between. A 'dead' case is one in which all the case information is presented to students at the start of the case analysis. To make a case 'live' a way has to be found to inject further information into the case over time. This allows a case to develop in a more realistic way. Some cases have a number of versions which describe different problem situations in the same organization at the same time. Students can build up their knowledge of the organization and its problems and develop increasingly sophisticated answers. Other cases allow for additional units of information to be added to the case over time. Sometimes this information is given; sometimes it has to be specifically asked for.

The truly 'live' case can take one of two forms. In the first form a member of the organization describes an existing situation in outline. Students must then ask questions in order to fill in what they feel are the relevant details. Clearly the case will be different each time it is taught. The second form involves a written description as in the conventional case method. However, students are then allowed to become involved in the actual situation collecting further information as they see fit. In this form the live case comes close to another learning method—the project. The main difference lies in the nature of the relationship between the organization and the students. A project would normally involve a student group recommending a course of action to members of the organization. A live case would tend to use the organization mainly as a source of information.

The more 'live' a case becomes the more realistic it is. Its potential for effective learning also increases. However 'live' cases require a level of skill that the beginning student does not possess. Most case leaders prefer to use this kind of case instruction as a bridge between a traditional case course and real world projects.

Even using a conventional written case there are a number of ways in which cases may be used. Figure 1.1 illustrates some of the alternatives. Examinations using cases are becoming more and more popular not only to assess case courses but also to evaluate the overall performance of students graduating from a course. In most situations cases are distributed some time before the examination. Students then analyse the case and bring their notes to the examination where they are required to answer three or four questions. Occasionally students may be asked to analyse, in three hours, a very short and straightforward case that they have not seen before.

Case courses usually make use of one of two methods in the classroom. The traditional Harvard method is an open class discussion. An alternative approach is to ask individuals or groups to make formal oral presentations of their case analyses and recommendations. This may or may not be followed by a general discussion. This method is easier to control than open discussions and fits the conventional timetable rather better. It also allows students practice at communicating their thoughts clearly. Unfortunately it tends to be less dynamic than the traditional Harvard method. Most learning takes place outside the classroom. It also allows students to minimize the effort they put in since they will usually only be involved in one or two presentations per course.

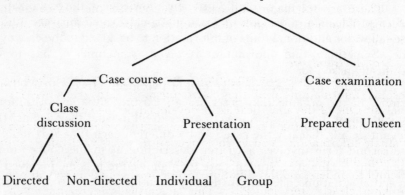

Figure 1.1 Alternative Methods of Using Cases

In the class discussion a major factor is the extent to which the case instructor directs the discussion. This direction may begin when the case is handed out. The case instructor may ask the students to direct their attention to a number of questions he would like answered. He may even specify which analytical techniques are to be used. A directive case instructor will control the flow of the discussion and ask specific students for their contributions. He may finish by outlining his solution to the case.

A non-directive case instructor will usually ask the question, 'What do you think are the major problems here?' at the beginning of the session. From then on he will chair the discussion, ask for clarification, agreement or disagreement. He will control the process of the discussion but not its content. Case instructors will normally expect written case analyses from individuals or groups. These may be handed in at the end of the session. Alternatively students may be allowed to refine them in the light of the case discussion and hand them in at a later date.

Each of these methods of case discussion and presentation has its own communication problems. Guidelines for tackling them will be given in chapters 12 and 13.

1.3 SKILLS DEVELOPED BY THE CASE METHOD

The case method is primarily a vehicle for developing skills; skills which are a vital part of a decision-maker's armoury. However these skills, by themselves, are not sufficient to make a good decision-maker. Harvard MBAs have been criticized, on occasions, for treating real world problems like case studies. There are major differences. Cases are one way in which instructors can provide a simulated environment in which to practise and develop skills. There is little at stake so students are free to experiment and learn. This is the strength of the case method, but also its weakness.

There are six major skill areas that the case method can help to develop. Together they can be described in one phrase—creative problem solving.

(a) Analytical skills
Case studies comprise information or, more properly, data. Data do not become information until they have meaning and relevance for the analyst. One of the analytical skills developed by the case method therefore is that of information handling. You learn to classify, organize and evaluate information. You learn to recognize when vital information is missing and how it might be obtained. Using this information you attempt to understand the situation as described. In doing so you practise thinking clearly and logically. This is particularly taxing when the information is not of high quality.

(b) Application skills
At a slightly lower level of difficulty the case method provides you with practice at applying concepts, techniques and principles. For example, techniques like discounted cash flow, decision theory and multiple

regression can be used to help students in their analysis. The key word is
help. Techniques like these cannot provide a solution by themselves. In
addition you learn to judge which techniques are appropriate, when they
may be used and how they fit in with less precise methods of analysis.

(c) Creative skills

Cases cannot be solved by logical processes alone. Creativity is vital to
good quality case presentations. This is not widely understood. Many
students who are afraid of quantitative methods but who nevertheless
pride themselves on their creativity, are frightened of cases. They must
realize that they have a vital skill necessary to good case work. They
should have the courage to play to their strengths while remedying their
weaknesses. Creativity is particularly important in generating alternative
solutions to the problems uncovered by logical analysis. It also helps when
trying to predict the outcomes that could result from following a
particular course of action.

(d) Communication skills

What communication skills are developed will depend on the way in
which the case leader chooses to run his class. You can learn to present
findings orally, to use visual aids and other media, to co-operate in group
presentations, to defend your own viewpoint, to convince others of your
arguments and to write clear and well-constructed reports.

(e) Social skills

Case discussions are essentially social processes. You can learn to communicate, listen, support, argue, guide and control yourself. Above all
you should gain a better understanding of your own behaviour and of that
of others in a loosely structured social situation. Many students have said
that in case courses they learned more about human behaviour than
about problem solving. This is particularly true if the class is split into
work groups and they give separate, competitive presentations.

(f) Self-analysis skills

Frequently disagreements occur in case discussions over value judgments
rather than analytical judgments. Cases provide a useful forum for
analysing your values. Would you really dismiss someone if you knew he
could not get another job? If a bribe was necessary to get a foreign
contract, would you pay it? It is certainly better to decide what you
believe in before you get into the firing line. You may be surprised how
much moral and ethical issues complicate what would otherwise be simple
decisions. Your instructor may deliberately use a case the central issue of
which is an ethical dilemma. This type of case usually generates the most
active, and heated, participation.

While the case method teaches skills, it can also impart knowledge. Over a case course students study a wide range of organizations. Much of his knowledge sticks. This can be a particularly important argument for using the case method with inexperienced students.

Instructors, by the way in which they teach, can emphasize certain skills at the expense of others. That is their right: they see the educational priorities. However, you should be aware of what it is possible to learn—by doing so you are likely to make case analysis a richer experience for yourself.

1.4 LEARNING PROBLEMS WITH THE CASE METHOD

The list of skills that can be learned by means of the case method is impressive. Perhaps too impressive. It is clear that the case method is very different from traditional teaching methods—the lecture, seminar or tutorial. Many students find the transition between the two very difficult to achieve. These are some of the problems they meet:

(a) What are we supposed to do?
There are three aspects to this dilemma. Firstly, students are not told what the problem is. They have to find it for themselves. Previously, it had always been clear what their goal was—learn a fact, apply a technique. Now they have to define their own goals. Worse still, even when they get an answer they are told that there is no unique solution. They cannot tell whether they are right or not. To cap it all, the information they have to work with is not cut and dried. It is sometimes ambiguous, sometimes irrelevant and sometimes it is not there at all. Students often describe their first few case discussions as like being in a fog without a compass. All their hard-won study skills are no longer applicable. It can be a disheartening experience.

(b) What are we learning?
After a lecture a student knows he has learned some facts. He knows that there are more facts in his notes that he can learn. He feels he has achieved something. He has learned. After a case discussion a student may feel that he has learned nothing. He may despair at the rambling and seemingly inefficient discussion process. He may feel he is no further forward. This is mainly due to the fact that improvements in the higher level skills that the case method promotes are difficult to detect. The individual may not be aware that he is progressing. Only by taking a longer term view will it be possible to be really sure that results are being achieved. Unfortunately, students may drop out—at least in terms of commitment to case analysis—before this occurs.

(c) Why doesn't the teacher teach?

Students frequently find the role of the case leader hard to understand. In their previous experience teachers taught and lecturers lectured. In a case discussion case leaders appear to refuse to do either. In particular they refuse to tell students what is correct and what is incorrect. Students are therefore cut off from a vital source of feedback. They are left to their own judgement or that of their peers.

The combination of these problems can be a devastating one. Students may feel helpless, disoriented, demotivated, and ultimately bored and resentful. Yet this need not be the case. Case instructors feel, quite rightly, that students should have to face complex, ambiguous situations and learn how to cope with them. They should not, however, be asked to do so without any help or outside guidance. That is not to say that they should be drilled in mechanical procedures to produce standard case analyses: there is a happy medium. Providing students with broad and flexible guidelines helps them to get over the initial shock of total immersion in the case method. It also provides a base from which they can build their own personal case analysis style. The rest of the book sets out such a system of guidelines. They have been tested and they work. Read on and see how they can improve your case analysis skills.

CHAPTER 2

A Step by Step Approach

2.1 RATIONALE

In order to understand each step of the approach the whole process is described in this chapter in outline. In addition, suggestions for learning to use the approach are discussed. Before doing this, however, it might be worth describing where this approach originated. Most papers and books on complex problem solving describe a similar approach. The basic ideas in different combinations have been around for a long time. However, two important adaptations have been made.

Firstly, an attempt has been made to take concepts, theories and principles from the literature on complex problem solving and combine them in a set of practical guidelines. This wasn't an easy task. It may be that in the process, some ideas have been distorted: that isn't too important. If the guidelines are relevant and practical, then that justifies what has been done. Secondly, the approach has been specifically tailored to the case method. Complex problems differ in all sorts of ways. By concentrating on the kinds of problems that arise in case studies, a more specific and therefore useful approach is possible.

2.2 THE SEVEN STEPS

Step 1. Understanding the situation

The basic meat of a case study is information. In the first step you must become familiar with this information and begin to work on it. The information should be organized to help you understand it and help you locate it easily later. The information contained in the case also needs evaluation. Not all of the information is valid, precise, or relevant. Vital pieces are missing. You will need to extrapolate from what is given if you are to make any decisions at all.

Step 2. Diagnosing problem areas

A problem is defined as the difference between what is (or will be) and

9

what we would like the situation to be. In this step you will be attempting to uncover these differences in the case situation. This is not altogether easy. Sometimes problems are simply symptoms of more fundamental problems. Sometimes problems are caused by a number of factors. Sometimes basic problems can lead to any number of symptoms. In this step you will be attempting to unravel these relationships. You will state the problems as precisely as you can and will relate them to each other. Not all problems are equally important. As your last task in this step, you will have to decide which problem (or problems) gets priority and why.

Step 3. Generating alternative solutions

This is a creative step. You need to understand, however, the nature of alternative solutions before you begin to use a variety of methods to think them up. This process could produce an enormous number of alternatives. There must therefore be some process of ranking alternatives in terms of their level. Major strategic alternatives must be examined first. When a decision has been made among them, it then makes sense to examine tactical alternatives. This may involve cycling through steps 4, 5 and 6 a number of times.

Step 4. Predicting outcomes

The first stage in choosing among alternatives is to predict what would happen if a particular alternative solution was put into action. Two particular warnings are important here. The first is to be sure to predict all the possible outcomes. It may be that a particular solution solves one problem only at the expense of creating another. Secondly, predicting is a difficult and uncertain business. Not all outcomes are equally likely to occur. You should be aware of the techniques which attempt to cope with the risk and uncertainty associated with a particular action.

Step 5. Evaluating alternatives

In this stage you will choose among the alternatives. This starts with the listing of pros and cons for each. In a series of stages these may be elaborated, qualified, and quantified to allow direct comparisons to be made. The choice is then made.

Step 6. Rounding out the analysis

Step 6 forms a bridge between the case analysis and communicating the results of that analysis. It involves making a decision about how many times you wish to cycle through stages 4 to 6 or, in other words, how much detail you wish to include. Events may not always turn out as you hope. A way of coping with this is contingency planning. It helps to add breadth as well as depth to your solution.

Step 7. Communicating the results

Your task does not end with a successfully completed case analysis. You must be prepared to undertake quite a bit more work planning how to communicate it. Chapters 12 and 13 cover oral and written communication using a traditional communication framework. Suffice it to say that there are more factors to take into account when designing a case presentation than most students realize.

2.3 USING THIS APPROACH

At this point it seems a useful idea to give some general advice on how to use this approach even before you fully understand it. One important psychological point to start with: it takes more time to read about the approach than to apply it, so don't be discouraged by the amount of material facing you. Once you have grasped the main points, the detail will fall into place.

Start by reading chapters 3 to 11 fairly quickly to get an overall appreciation of the ideas being presented. Try to grasp the essentials rather than worry about the detail. You will notice that what is described is a very complete approach to case analysis. You may not be ready for this degree of complexity yet. Because of this problem, at the end of each chapter or pair of chapters there is a section called *Guide to Use*. This section discusses which procedures are basic and which may be regarded as optional, at least in the early stages of learning the case method.

Choose a short case and try out the procedures described. In each chapter read the *Guide to Use* first and decide which procedures you think will be most useful at your next stage of development. Compare your results with the examples given in the text to make sure you can apply the ideas correctly. As your case experience increases try out the optional procedures. You should find that they help you to continue improving your analytical skills.

When you are still a beginner, you may find that you have to cycle back to earlier steps in the process because you missed a problem or failed to see a particularly attractive solution. Don't worry too much about this. However, you should beware of missing out steps. This is a 'building up from the foundations' approach. You may find that your finished work does not stand up to criticism if you have not laid the groundwork well. You may also notice that different cases will make varying demands on different steps of the process. This is only to be expected. In recognizing this you are beginning to develop as a case analyst.

In the long term, the aim must be to develop your own approach. The approach described here is not meant to be a mechanical set of procedures to be followed *ad nauseam*. It is meant to bridge the gap between the complete novice and the skilled practitioner. Your own personal case work style might incorporate elements from this approach or it may be completely different. The objective of this book is simply to get you over the initial learning hurdles so that you can develop in your own way.

CHAPTER 3

Step One:
Understanding the
Situation (I)

Step one involves trying to understand the case situation without prejudging it. This is achieved through the twin processes of organizing and evaluating the information.

3.1 CASE EXAMPLES

There is no better way to understand the application of a principle or concept than by concrete example. For this reason each major chapter in the book which describes a step in the case analysis process is introduced by a short case. They will be used as the source of most of the illustrations used in the text. With the exception of the Spanline Engineering case they have all been written especially for this book.

You will need to be reasonably familiar with each case as you read the chapter that follows it. You should read the example case through at least twice before you proceed. In addition refer back to the case whenever examples are used so that you can see how they occur in context. A word of warning is necessary. Only one aspect of any one case is tackled in a particular chapter. The analyses are therefore incomplete. You shouldn't be tempted to judge that that is all there is to that case. These cases are being used primarily as a source of illustration and example.

On the other hand each case is complete in its own right. You can use them to practise your case analysis skills and I encourage you to do so. Although the cases are short they illustrate one of the major strengths of the case method. They contain enough material to keep you occupied for many hours. Lots of different issues are touched upon and as a set they cover most management functions.

Kennetson Printers Ltd.

On the 1st January 1979, Noel McKinny was made managing director of

13

Kennetson Printers Ltd.(KPL), a small general printing firm situated on the outskirts of a West Midlands town. KPL had recently been acquired by ICAL (Industrial Holdings) Ltd. along with a number of other companies which made up Linkletter and Cross Ltd., a loosely structured industrial holding company. ICAL had bought the group in order to gain control of two of its profitable engineering companies. They had succeeded in selling off or closing down another seven companies but failed to find a buyer for KPL. It continued to make modest profits (see exhibit 3.3) and ICAL were loth to close it down especially in an area of high unemployment. Accordingly Noel McKinny, assistant to the group managing director, was asked to take over the running of KPL.

McKinny's remit was clear. He was to build up the company's operations until such time as it could be profitably sold or else prove itself a viable part of ICAL. By early March of 1979 McKinny had had time to familiarize himself with KPL's operations and he was about to call a management committee meeting to tell them what he intended to do.

KPL had been founded by John Kennetson in the 1930s as a small jobbing printing company. By the time it was acquired by Linkletter Ltd., in the late 1950s, the company had made the transition from a family firm to an industrial company with professional management. Kennetson left the company when he sold it to Linkletter Ltd., but his general manager George Shellcross stayed on until the ICAL takeover, at which time he retired.

KPL specialized in quality letterpress and litho printing and much of its equipment was modern and efficient. It had a full range of facilities including a small design studio. Industrial relations in the plant were reasonably good though the sales director attributed this to the fact that they had 'bought the unions off time and time again'. He would usually go on to say that it would have to stop sometime.

There were 93 people employed in the factory of whom five were in a supervisory capacity. The sales, design, general administration and accounting offices accounted for 24 people and there were four salesmen. Under Noel McKinny there were three directors: finance, production and sales. He had interviewed each of them several times during January and February 1979 and much of the information he needed to make his first decisions came from them.

Richard Gaskin, the finance director, was something of a surprise. He was 34 and as well as being a chartered accountant had graduated from a British business school with an MBA. He had joined KPL about a year before the takeover. Gaskin was not impressed by KPL's performance or by its accounting system. He had spent the last year doing something about the latter, and he now expected McKinny to do something about the former. He saw no critical problem areas; in his view everything needed improving 'by about 20% to 25%'.

David Elwes, the production director, was approaching retiring age. He had worked in KPL all his life and was an expert in printing techniques. He still kept up to date with printing developments and regularly travelled to conferences, exhibitions and conferences in the UK and in Europe. He told Noel McKinny, 'I leave most of the day to day detail to the factory manager and the shift supervisors. We are probably one of the few printing companies around making any sort of money. That's because we can handle any kind of job no matter how technically difficult. That's not to say we don't do run of the mill stuff: we do. But what we are known for is our technical skills. Our blokes take a pride in their work. There are few printing shops in the country that can touch us.' Elwes felt that the only problems they had were typical of Britain in the late 1970s. He fervently hoped that ICAL would leave them alone to get on with their job.

Alex Pendlebury was in his mid forties and had only recently returned to work after a heart attack. Although he ate less and jogged every day he still worked long hours and clocked up hundreds of miles in his company car every month. Pendlebury explained that KPL was largely a jobbing printer although at the quality end of the market. Richard Gaskin had been able to produce for him some sales analyses by major types of business and by customer size (exhibits 3.1 and 3.2) but he had not had time to look at them in detail yet. They would give McKinny an idea of the business.

	Sales	Contribution
Catalogues	593	403
Brochures/promotional material	336	218
Technical literature	315	198
Periodicals	196	157
Calendars	187	127
Company reports	175	131
Magazine printing	157	105
Miscellaneous	417	243
	2,376	1,582

Exhibit 3.1 Sales and Contribution Analysis by Major Types of Business (1978/79) (£ 000's)

Annual purchase size (£ 000's)	Number of customers
30+	5
20-29	21
10-19	48
5-9	83
0-4	171
	328

Exhibit 3.2 Sales Analysis by Customer Purchase Size (1978/79)

	Sales (£ 000's)	Profit (£ 000's)
1968	1286	82
1969	1447	133
1970	1608	125
1971	1614	74
1972	1699	136
1973	1798	149
1974	1914	145
1975	2015	177
1976	2076	137
1977	2260	188
1978	2376	180

Exhibit 3.3 Eleven-Year Sales and Profit Growth

'I handle the major accounts which are mostly in and around the West Midlands though there are significant customers in London. The four representatives each have a territory—London and the South, West Midlands and Wales, East Midlands and East Anglia, North of England and Scotland. In our type of business it's mostly keeping existing customers happy. New business comes to us because of our reputation. Any potential customer will come to us eventually. It's our job to make sure he stays with us.'

Pendlebury was mainly concerned about prices. He and his salesmen seemed to do nothing but tell customers about price increases. Instead of selling they were apologizing all the time. KPL had to find ways of holding the line on price. Standing up to the unions would be one way. Stopping the purchase of ever more expensive printing gadgets and machines would be another.

Noel McKinny had developed some views about KPL's operations and how they might be improved. He had, up to now, been employed in ICAL in a number of staff functions, mostly with a high analytical content. He was looking forward to trying out his ideas in a situation where he decided rather than advised. The next meeting of the management committee would be an ideal forum.

	£	£
Net sales	2,376,042	
Closing work in progress	46,470	
		2,422,512
Opening work in progress		59,761
Output		2,362,751
Cost of output:		
Production		
Factory wages	895,164	
Factory management	52,791	
Depreciation	126,742	
Other expenses	128,264	
	1,202,961	
Materials	682,946	
		1,885,907
Overhead costs:		
Selling		
Salaries and commission	46,254	
Expenses	37,942	
		84,196
Distribution and transport		34,177
Administration		
Management salaries	61,746	
Staff salaries	146,942	
Administrative expenses	58,060	
		178,902
		2,183,182
Operating profit		**179,569**

Exhibit 3.4 Kennetson Printers Ltd, Summary Profit and Loss Account, Year Ended 1, October 1978

	£	£
Fixed assets		
Plant, machinery, fixtures and fittings	893,301	
Property	84,872	
Vehicles	36,942	
		1,015,115
Current assets		
Stocks	113,672	
Work in progress	264,922	
Debtors	420,763	
Cash	1,500	
	800,857	
Current liabilities		
Creditors	212,326	
Bank overdraft	110,946	
Corporation tax	62,342	
Ordinary dividend	36,429	
	422,043	
Net current assets		378,814
Net assets employed		1,393,929
Sources of capital		
Ordinary shares		350,000
Reserves		531,738
Loan capital		120,000
Deferred taxation		42,191

Exhibit 3.5 Kennetson Printers Ltd, Summary Balance Sheet, Year Ended 1, October 1978

3.2 INITIAL READING

The first step is to skim-read the case. This means that you do not stop to re-read things you may not have understood or to highlight things you think important. Your objective is to try and comprehend what is in the case. After this first reading you should be able to describe in your own words what the case is about.

If at all possible read the case for the first time in a situation when you know you won't be able to do much more than read it through. This allows the material to 'mature' in your head until the time for the real work arrives. It is quite incredible how much you will have retained and how much of the initial work will have been already done by your unconscious. This procedure also prevents a feeling of frustration. In the early stages of analysis, you will find yourself reading and re-reading sections of the case. It is easy to create an information overload which then leads to boredom making the analysis that much more difficult. Spreading the process out makes the whole thing more enjoyable.

Read the case in the first instance like a cheap novel. Don't try to evaluate. Don't begin to decide what the problems might be. Suspend your judgement until a later stage. You cannot really begin to analyse the case until you know what all the evidence is. Leaping to premature conclusions may mean you undervalue vital clues or miss them altogether. For the same reasons try to give equal attention to every bit of information. Those boring looking appendices may be the core of the case.

3.3 ORGANIZING THE INFORMATION

3.3.1 Objectives

Your objectives in organizing the information in the case are to help you to understand the situation described. The process of organizing, i.e. working with the information, also helps you to memorize or at least know it exists and where it is in the case. The end product of this organization process should be a compact picture of the case situation, in your head and on paper. Again, it should be emphasized that what you are aiming for is description and understanding. Don't begin to look for problems or solutions. However, if a really brilliant insight hits you during this process note it down for subsequent following up. Don't allow it to become a red herring. A systematic approach is the only way you can be sure of doing a thorough analysis.

There are a number of ways in which you can organize the information in a case. Here are five which you may find useful.

3.3.2 Indexing

In long cases it frequently helps to compile an index to the case material. This serves to highlight the easy-to-forget areas like appendices and illustrations. There is no real need to do this for the Kennetson Printing Ltd. case but an index for this case might look like this:

> The takeover
> McKinny's remit
> Decision situation
> Company history
> Production facilities
> People
> Finance director's comments
> Production director's comments
> Sales director's comments
> McKinny's decision situation
> Balance sheet
> Profit and Loss Account
> Sales by product
> Sales by customer size

This may immediately suggest whole areas of information that are missing. You should note what these might be. What to do about missing information is discussed in section 4.1.3.

Indexing can be taken a stage further by the use of cross-references. Any section in the case may deal with several topics. For a particularly complex case it is sometimes useful to cross-reference the sequence or contents list against another index. For example in the Kennetson case the first paragraph gives some information on McKinny, ICAL, Linkletter and Cross, KPL, etc. Information on any of these topics might be required in the later stages of analyses so that it would be useful to know where it is. This suggests another way of developing the information in the case.

3.3.3 Restructuring

Cases are normally written so that they are easy to read. This often means that they are structured in ways which are not necessarily the most useful for analytic purposes. For example, a historical write-up may discuss the personality of the managing director in several different time periods. It would help to understand the situation better if all of these pieces of information were grouped together. For example, this is some of the information relating to Noel McKinny.

Noel McKinny
Newly-appointed managing director of KPL
Previously assistant to the Group Managing Director of ICAL
Quick to take decisive action?
Consults fellow directors
Previously only in staff positions
Analytical skills
Ambitious

Restructuring may be carried out in two ways. First the nature of the case may be used to suggest what categories you would use for restructuring. In the Kennetson case there is quite a lot of information about the four people involved. It would make sense to collect the information on each individual and perhaps compare them. A second category might be the nature of ICAL; a third might be the market for KPL's products; a fourth the industrial relations situation. These are all topics suggested by the information in the case.

An alternative method of restructuring is to bring to the case an analytical framework; either a general one or one specific to the discipline you are studying. An example of a general framework is that originated by Kenneth Schnelle which relates mainly to organizational case studies. It has three broad categories into which the information in a case can be placed.

(a) Organizational—to do with the organization's position with respect to other organizations, its structure and its goals and objectives.

(b) Operations—to do with how the organization currently operates: this category is subdivided into the main functional areas—planning, control, etc.

(c) History—to do with past actions, decisions and policies and their results which have led up to the current situation.

If you were studying personnel, marketing or production, the following frameworks would be appropriate.

Personnel	*Marketing*	*Production*
Industrial relations	Marketing organization	Management systems
Manpower planning	Consumer behaviour	Facilities planning
Recruitment and selection	Market characteristics	Production scheduling
Employment	Market segments	Inventory control
Training	Price	Quality control

Management development	Product	Work performance
Performance appraisal	Distribution channels	Human engineering
Pay	Advertising and promotion	
Health and safety		

Accountants, design engineers, architects and educational technologists all have similar frameworks. They may be as simple as a list of variables that theorists have discovered to be useful in describing the phenomena they habitually study; they may be as complex as a well articulated theory, e.g. Howard's consumer behaviour model. In each case you have to decide whether that framework is a useful way of organizing the information in a case. The key criterion is whether it results in better understanding.

A useful by-product of restructuring the information is that it quickly reveals what is missing. For example in the Kennetson case there is no mention of consumer behaviour, capital funding or wage negotiation procedures. These may or may not be vital to a complete understanding of the situation. However the use of a discipline-based framework as a check-list at least ensures that you are made more aware of areas of ignorance.

3.3.4 Extending

Extending may be regarded as the stage beyond restructuring. Extending means to combine information in ways that create new information and hence improve understanding. Here are some of the ways of extending the information in the Kennetson case.

The order in which events occur and the intervals between events are often crucial in understanding a case. A chronology can be a useful way in which to sort out temporal relationships.

1930s	Started operation
late 1950s	Acquisition by Linkletter
1 January 1979	Acquisition by ICAL
Early March 1979	Decisions to be made by McKinny

Table 3.1 Chronology for the Kennetson Case

The Kennetson case does not have a complex time dimension. Nevertheless the chronology illustrates the point that McKinny will be eeking to make changes, after a short acquaintance with the company, against a background of long tradition and stable operation.

Tabulation is the process of collecting together information from different sources and displaying it together in the belief that greater understanding will be the end result. In the Kennetson case this can be done for the number of employees in different functions.

Department	Numbers	%
Factory	88	70
Factory management	5	4
Sales	4	3
Directors	4	3
Other administrative personnel	24	20
	125	100

Table 3.2 Number of Employees by Department

This tabulation raises more questions than it answers. What proportion of the factory employees are on shift work? What functional divisions, such as quality and production control, are there within the factory? How many people are there in accounts? The design studio? Nevertheless by pulling all the information together it helps the analyst to get a clearer picture of the type of operation that Kennetson comprises. In addition it provides a good basis upon which to make assumptions should this prove to be necessary later in the analysis.

Tabulations can often only be expressed in restricted form. Sales must be at least . . ., or costs must be greater than. . . . For example in the Kennetson case the size of the design studio is greater than one person and fewer than 24. If one wished to make reasonable assumptions about the size of the other departments in administration then this range could be very much reduced. Information in this restricted form—the figure lies between X and Y—is obviously not as instructive as we would like it to be. Nevertheless it is still useful information. Students often baulk at making the rather cumbersome calculations involved; they do not realize that they can reduce the uncertainty in the data quite considerably by using this technique. And any method by which more pieces of the jigsaw can be slotted into place should not be ignored.

Graphic extensions of the information available in the case can provide useful insights. The organization chart (figure 3.1) is a useful way of summarizing the structure of an organization.

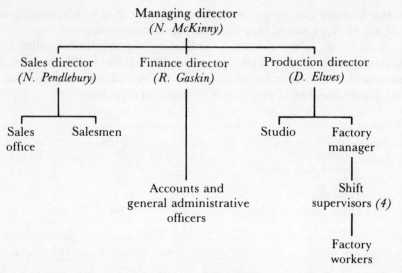

Figure 3.1 Kennetson Printers Ltd., Organization Chart

Maps may be used to sketch out geographical information such as factory locations, distribution networks and sales force territories. This can lead to surprising results. Few people are accurate judges of geographical distance or areas. Diagrams or sketches can provide insights about the layout of a factory floor or the form and function of a product. In each case you would be abstracting information from the case and rearranging it in order to create new and additional information.

3.3.5 Summarizing

Summarizing is almost the reverse of extending. There are an enormous number of data, qualitative and quantitative, in a case. Summarizing is a process which you will be doing continually throughout your case analysis. In familiarizing yourself with the case you will need to begin this process.

But first it is necessary to sound a note of warning. Summarizing means throwing away information. An average is an excellent summarizing device for many forms of quantitative data but it hides any variation there may be between individual figures. At this early stage you cannot be sure that the information hidden in a summary is not vital to your analysis. For example you might jot down in your notes, 'ICAL is an aggressive, results-orientated, commercially minded industrial holding company'. Yet one of the reasons given for not closing KPL down was that it was situated in an area of high unemployment. Similarly the average customer size is £7,240 but there are several over £30,000 and quite a few order less than £4,000 a year. In practice there are relatively few customers of an average size! You should not be seduced into thinking in terms of this mythical 'average customer' when, for example, you consider giving bulk discounts.

Quantitative summary

Quantitative data are much easier to summarize than qualitative data. There are rules for combining numbers and the main judgement comes in deciding which summary technique to apply to which set of data. Means, medians or modes may be used to give an indication of central location in data sets. Standard deviation or interquartile range may be used as measures of dispersion. Ehrenberg's *Data Reduction* (see *Further Reading* for details), is an excellent and unusual introduction to this topic.

Let us look at exhibits 3.1, 3.2 and 3.3 and see how they might be summarized. Exhibit 3.1 analyses both sales and contribution by the major types of business the company does. It would obviously make no sense to calculate the average sales per type of business. The categories are not particularly clearly defined and the miscellaneous group probably contains a vast array of other types of business. The average amount of sales per sector or market is less important than how those sales are distributed among the sectors. A simple way of investigating this would be to calculate what percentage of the total sales falls within each sector. This has been done incrementally and cumulatively in table 3.3.

	Incremental %	Cumulative %
Catalogues	25	25
Brochures/promotional material	14	39
Technical literature	13	52
Periodicals	8	60
Calendars	8	68
Company reports	7	75
Magazine printing	7	82
Miscellaneous	7	100
	100	

Table 3.3 Percentage of Sales by Major Types of Business

Over 50% of sales are accounted for by three business sectors. This is not an evaluative statement but simply a summary statement of fact. It may indicate 'too many eggs in too few baskets' or else a carefully considered specialization strategy. You should not begin to think in these terms at this stage of your analysis. Simply note the facts and move on. Problem finding comes later.

A more elaborate analysis might involve comparing categories not by size as in table 3.3 but by the nature of the business involved. For example periodical and magazine printing (15% of sales) is likely to be regular business at weekly, monthly or quarterly intervals. Catalogues, calendars and company reports (40% of sales) are likely to involve annual contracts perhaps concentrated at certain peak times of the year. Brochures and technical literature orders (27% of sales) can turn up at any time. Many of KPL's sales leads appear to be predictable in terms of time and customer. There are implications here for sales force organization and factory loading. This is an example of trying to wring out every ounce of meaning from the data available.

Exhibit 3.2 allows us to examine the distribution of customer size. The average customer purchased £7,240 worth of printing from KPL in 1978/79. However as in most distributions of this kind a large number of small customers is balanced by a small number of very large customers. The average is therefore not a very good summary. A better summary statement would be '1.5% of customers account for at least 6% of sales'. By making assumptions about where the mean purchase size lies in each size category (it will usually be nearer the lower limit) it would be possible to calculate what percentage of customers accounted for what percentage of sales. This measures how concentrated KPL's business is in customer terms. Again, no judgements should be made. You are, at this stage, simply trying to understand KPL and its operations.

Exhibit 3.3 once again illustrates the limits of a straightforward average. Clearly sales, and to a lesser extent profits, have been steadily increasing over the period. Average sales or profits over the 11 years hardly captures the essential information contained in the table. What is needed is some way of summarizing the trends. The average percentage rise in sales and profits does this. The figures are 6% for sales and 6% for profits. Once again, however, the average hides as much as it reveals. Annual percentage sales increases have only varied from 0.4% to 11%. Annual percentage profit increases have oscillated from −68.9% to +45.6%. Comparison of these ranges quite nicely summarizes KPL's sales and profit growth over the last eleven years.

Exhibits 3.1, 3.2 and 3.3 have been examined in a number of different ways. These by no means exhaust the possibilities particularly if the analyst is prepared to make a few more assumptions. The point is that you should not mechanically apply the quantitative techniques that you have been taught. Always in the forefront of your mind you should keep two questions. What do these quantitative data tell me about the situation I am analysing? How can these data be summarized so that I can clearly and unambiguously communicate them to someone else?

Qualitative summary
Qualitative data are less easy to summarize. Students frequently tend to

leap to conclusions and make broad generalizations based on very little information. That is why summaries of qualitative data should be carefully worded and qualified where necessary. For example at first glance Noel McKinny appears to be an ambitious, aggressive and dynamic man out to make a name for himself at KPL. Yet he has spent two months getting to know the business and making relationships with the three directors. A less patient man might have wanted to put his stamp on the operation very much sooner. These facts might be summarized in the following way.

> Noel McKinny's personality—keen, ambitious. Wants to run his own show, intelligent and analytical, but probably wants to take others along with him. Not really aggressive or ruthless.

Summarizing the data in a case is a necessity. You cannot keep all the data in your head, retrieving it only when it is required. In addition, summarizing provides insights that are not necessarily obvious when you are immersed in detail. It allows you to see the wood for the trees. But an earlier warning needs repeating. Summarize, but don't forget where the summaries came from. Don't hesitate to go back to the original data in order to resolve contradictions or clarify key issues as they occur in later stages of your analysis.

3.3.6 Relating

Relating is the process by which relationships between variables are uncovered. This is one of the most important ways in which understanding of a situation is promoted. Isolated facts or summaries, even groups of related facts, are useful building blocks. However relationships are the mortar that binds these blocks together to make a coherent and valid structure. For example it may be useful to note that productivity in a factory has increased not steadily but in a series of sharp steps. It is even more useful to discover that these steps coincide with bonus payments rather than with the conclusion of productivity agreements. A relationship has been tentatively identified. In the familiarization stage of case analysis that is all that is required. They will be used as the raw material for the building of more complex structures in the next phase of analysis. Think of the process of establishing relationships as one of prefabricating parts for use in subsequent building operations.

Qualitative relationships
Relationships involving qualitative data are more difficult to establish than relationships among quantified variables. Nevertheless it is possible to identify possible relationships. For example David Elwes, the production director of KPL is mainly interested in technical matters and

'leave(s) the day to day detail to the factory manager . . .'. Could this be the reason why the sales director, Alex Pendlebury, accused the company of buying the unions off? The two variables are (a) management uninterested or unskilled in negotiation and industrial relations and (b) high wage and salary increases. They clearly coexist in KPL at the current time but does one thing cause the other? And does it do so by itself? The only way to test the relationship would be to vary (a) by replacing or retraining Elwes. All that can be said at the moment is that a possible relationship exists.

The fact that variables are not always quantified obviously makes the teasing out of relationships difficult. Another source of difficulty is that few relationships are confined to just two variables. This means that multivariable analysis is required. Frequently the data in the case are not capable of supporting analysis of this kind. For example you may wish to discover which variables correlate with total sales volume. Two of the variables you choose are quantified, but one is quantified for a much shorter period than the other. Another two variables are only available as qualitative data. Finally the three remaining variables have not been measured at all or if they have the data are not contained in the case.

In this sort of situation you have to be content with squeezing what you can out of what is available. You must not expect too much of two or even three variable analyses. Other, unmeasured, variables will often get in the way and camouflage the relationship. However, at least in the first instance, you must treat the data as it is and not as you would like it to be.

Quantitative relationships
Exhibits 3.1 and 3.3 each contain data on two variables and the relationships are well worth examining. In Exhibit 3.1 the two variables are sales and contribution for each of the major types of business. The correlation between the two can be seen to be very strong simply by looking at the two columns of figures. Calculating the contribution to sales ratio for each category confirms the strength of the relationship. In table 3.4 these ratios are all close to 0.67. The relationship can be expressed in mathematical form as

$$\text{contribution} = 0.67 \text{ sales}$$

Clearly this is not a perfect fit. Some variation remains to be explained in terms of other variables. For example, periodicals have a higher than average contribution. This could be the result of the regularity and size of the business involved. Perhaps periodical publishers are willing to pay high prices in order to guarantee delivery. On the other hand it may be that volume purchases of paper and ink reduce costs. Miscellaneous business on the other hand has a low contribution margin. Could this be marginal business, priced low to fill capacity in slack periods? Could it be highly technical, developmental, specialized work on which it is impossible to fully recoup the high costs involved? All the above are really examples of multivariable analyses; bringing in a third variable to explain what variation is left when the second variable has been correlated with the first. A similar sort of analysis is possible using the data in table 3.4.

	Contribution/sales %	Difference from mean
Catalogues	68	+ 1
Brochures/promotional material	65	– 2
Technical literature	63	– 4
Periodicals	80	+ 13
Calendars	68	+ 1
Company reports	75	+ 8
Magazine printing	67	0
Miscellaneous	58	– 9
Mean	**67**	

Table 3.4 Contribution to Sales Ratios for Major Types of Business

Ratio analysis

A very different kind of analysis is possible using KPL's profit and loss account and balance sheet. This is a technique known as ratio analysis. By relating various accounting figures it is possible to build up a picture of the structure of a firm's operations as described by their accounting system. The structure can be very nicely illustrated by means of a pyramid of ratios. The pyramid shows how each facet of the business contributes towards the achievement of a key objective of any profit-making organization—return on capital. The pyramid for KPL is shown in figure 3.2. This is a somewhat simplified version used here only to illustrate the principles involved. For a more comprehensive treatment you should refer to P. Bird, *Understanding Company Accounts* (see the section entitled *Further Reading*, at the back of the book).

The operating profit to operating capital figure for KPL is around 10%. This is further broken down into two key ratios—operating profit to net sales and net sales to operating capital. The important thing to notice here is that these two ratios, when multiplied together, give the original return on capital ratio at the apex of the pyramid. In other words any change in profitability can only be achieved by a change in one or both of these ratios. This type of interrelationship operates throughout the pyramid. A change in any of the variables will result in a change in profitability unless there is an exactly counterbalancing change in another variable somewhere in the pyramid.

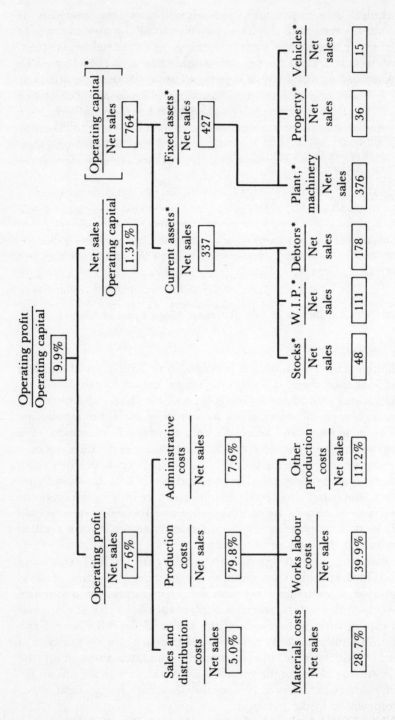

Figure 3.2 Pyramid of Ratios for KPL (1977/78)

* *Per £000 of net sales*

The left-hand branches of the pyramid describe the operating results of the firm. It reveals the balance between profit and the many categories of cost that are needed to generate it. For KPL the dominance of production costs, and within these, works labour costs, is very apparent.

The right-hand branches of the pyramid are concerned with the utilization of the capital assets of the company. The net sales to operating capital ratio is inverted at the apex of these right hand branches. This is simply a mathematical convenience. The components of operating capital can only be separated out if they form the numerator of a ratio. In addition the result is multiplied by 1,000 to give values per £1,000 of net sales. The first components of operating capital to be split off are current and fixed assets. The relationship between these two ratios is descriptive of the kind of operation that the firm is running. The fact that fixed assets loom larger than current assets in the asset structure supports the description of KPL as a well equipped firm with up-to-date machinery. At the next level plant and machinery do indeed form the major part of the fixed assets.

Completing a ratio pyramid like this gives a case analyst a very good feeling for the structure of a company's operations. It provides a well established framework within which to work and pin-points the relationships that are vital to understanding any commercial organization. It is also a very quick, though somewhat mechanical, method for organizing the accounting data which most cases contain. Finally it is the first stage in a process designed to uncover problems in a firm's operations. The differences between one firm's ratios and those of other firms operating in the same or similar industries afford clues as to that firm's strengths and weaknesses. When backed up with other evidence they form the basis for defining problem areas. They also offer hints of possible solutions. Problems and solutions are the themes of the next two chapters and ratio analysis will be discussed again in those contexts.

3.3.7 Highlighting

Students are often urged to go through a case 'highlighting the key pieces of information'. The availability of yellow highlight markers has done much to encourage this practice. But what is a key piece of information? Simply picking out what strikes you as interesting or important is an unsystematic way of tackling a case.

On its own it is both wasteful and dangerous. Highlighting is wasteful because you find that you finish up underlining every other sentence or figure. Reviewing what you have done you may feel that you do not understand the situation much better than when you started.

Highlighting is dangerous because it encourages premature judgement. For example in the early part of the Kennetson case the company is not described in particularly glowing terms. The following phrases can serve as examples; 'small general printing firm', 'failed to find a buyer for KPL', 'modest profit', 'loth to close it down especially in an area of high unemployment', 'founded in the 1930s'. You may decide that KPL is 'on the skids' and go on to look for and highlight evidence that supports that view. You might ignore or discount evidence to the contrary, such as the fact that the company has modern and efficient equipment. An early judgement may lead you to select only that information which fits your preconceived view. This is a major problem for students new to the case method. They wish to get on with the analysis and grab at the first idea that comes along. Highlighting only encourages this process which, needless to say, is not a good habit to acquire.

Highlighting is best used in conjunction with restructuring, extending, relating and summarizing. It provides a way of classifying information which you are then going to work on. For example, you could go through a case underlining all the information relating to profit and profitability. These data could then be worked on as required. In this situation you know before you start what you are looking for and why it is being highlighted. This not only makes your task easier but it also forms part of a systematic technique which you know is building towards a better understanding of the case situation.

CHAPTER 4

Step One: Understanding the Situation (II)

4.1 EVALUATING THE INFORMATION

4.1.1 Objectives

Up to now it has been assumed that all information is the same. This is clearly not the case. The information in a case differs quite considerably in a number of ways. Since information is the main substance of any case, it must be assessed and evaluated before and while it is being used. In a way information comprises the building blocks of a case analysis. You need to understand the nature and quality of the materials before you begin to build. Many a brilliant case analysis has fallen down because it was built upon shaky informational foundations.

The information in a case may be said to differ in at least three respects—precision, validity and relevance. Each are discussed below but it will be argued that only the first two have practical application at this stage of case analysis.

4.1.2 Precision

Precision refers to the degree of uncertainty implicit in a particular figure or statement. Precision is a continuous variable but for purposes of illustration a four-category system seems appropriate.

Degree of Precision	Kennetson Examples
Precise	The date McKinny joined Kennetson, company accounts, number of salesmen
Imprecise	'. . . much of the equipment was modern and efficient' 'Industrial relations in the plant were reasonably good . . .' 'much of the information he needed to make his early decisions came from them.'
Very imprecise	'. . . bought the unions off' 'We are probably one of the few printing companies around making any sort of money.'

Missing   prices, competitive analysis, factory layout, ICAL's time-
                               table.

Missing information is included in this classification because it represents
the ultimate in imprecision. It is a very important category and will be
discussed in some detail later in this chapter.

On the whole it is preferable to have more rather than less precise
information. For example you might build a strategy on the 'fact' that
'Industrial relations in the plant were reasonably good,' but how good is
'reasonably good'? Does it mean there have been no disputes or strikes,
only a few or simply less than in the rest of the printing industry? Your
view about which applies will make a substantial difference to the policies
you might recommend.

The problem is therefore to highlight imprecise information; precise
information can look after itself. Two procedures can be used to help. The
first is to read through the case especially in order to pick out imprecise
information. It will usually be too much trouble to note them all.
However you should be aware where they occur and be sensitive to their
use in subsequent analysis.

The second is to carry forward the imprecision into the later stages of
analysis. It is easy, for example, to summarize industrial relations as
being 'good' rather than 'reasonably good'. The qualification may make
all the difference in the world. It is very easy to forget how the information
was originally given. The usual tendency is for qualifications to be
forgotten and precision to increase as the analysis proceeds. This can lead
you to make unwarranted conclusions and should be avoided.

In the early stages when you are looking for the major problems and
devising solutions, precision may not be so much of a problem. These are
essentially exploratory processes and you may not care, or be able, to dot
every *i* and cross every *t*. However, when you come to evaluating and
choosing between alternative solutions, precision does become important
then. The difference between alternatives may hang on the precision of a
statement in the case text.

4.1.3 Improving precision and filling gaps

Cases are never solved solely on the information contained in the case. At
a minimum level case analysts import information concerning facts and
relationships which they believe reflect how the world works. That is to
say, they make assumptions which they believe are valid in the context of
the case. At the other end of the scale, case analysts may collect specific
information concerning the case situation and use this to augment what is
already there.

In both instances this is a response to imprecise or missing information. From the first stage of case analysis onwards, you will become aware of information gaps or concerned at the lack of clarity in some of the statements made. Since what is important will change as your analysis progresses, you may find that you may have to repeat the search for supplementary information a number of times. So, although collecting further information is discussed here, it may be relevant to any stage of the case analysis process.

The first thing to check is whether or not your case instructor will allow you to 'go outside the case'. In general they will probably encourage you to do so. It allows you to learn the skills of information collection as well as information processing. It also adds a dynamic dimension to the case method. Effectively, different students will be analysing different cases. However, problems can arise. Not all students may have equal access to information sources. It is also possible that students new to the case method will invest too much time searching and not enough in analysis. There is a tendency to believe that the answer is out there somewhere if only it can be found. A case instructor may want to discourage this attitude.

Why is it missing?
Having identified imprecise or missing information which you believe important to your understanding of the case, the next stage is to ask the key question, 'Why is it missing or incomplete?'. This must be considered before deciding how, if at all, the information could be obtained. In general, there are three possibilities.

First, it may be that the information is simply unobtainable. In the Kennetson case it would have been very useful to have an attitude survey of print buyers to see if Elwes's view of KPL's reputation was justified. It is highly unlikely that such a survey existed at the time the case was written.

Secondly it may be that the casewriter did not include the information although it was available to him. He may have made a conscious decision to exclude or qualify information because he thought it would make a better case. In the Kennetson case there are no details of the plant and machinery, competitors or product characteristics. Presumably the casewriter wished students to concentrate on the strategic and organizational aspects of the case.

It may be that the casewriter would have liked to include information but failed to do so. Sometimes casewriters are denied access to key pieces of information when writing cases; information which would have been readily available to decision-makers. At other times casewriters become so enmeshed in the process that they fail to realize that they have not collected vital information. Too often students think that because the information is not there it must be irrelevant. This is a very unwise assumption.

Although internal information of this kind may be available, you should not attempt to collect it. It cannot be stressed too firmly that students should not approach the organization described in the case. The organization has already been inconvenienced by allowing the casewriter access to people and data. They cannot be expected to be very happy about doing the same for every group of students who are assigned the case to analyse. For similar reasons, students should not attempt to uncover the identity of anonymous organizations described in a case.

Thirdly, there is information which is not included in the case most probably because the casewriter wished to keep the case short. This is likely to be mostly environmental information. For example, it might have been possible to discover if KPL was 'one of the few printing companies around making any sort of money'. This information may be obtained from reliable secondary sources. It is relatively easily available and cheap to collect. It does not directly involve the organization in the case. Whether it proves valuable or not will depend on the analytical skills of the case analyst.

Hindsight

One final point should be made concerning hindsight. In some instances it is possible to discover what actually happened to the organization or the industry after the point in time when the case is set. One situation may be that you know what decision was taken and what resulted from it. If this is so then you have more useful information than is normal in case analysis. You do not however have the solution. What would have happened had they made a different decision? Thus you can still analyse the case in the normal way. You are simply better informed than you would normally be. Hindsight helps in this instance but it should not determine the outcome.

A second situation occurs when a major and unpredictable change in the environment has happened since the time when the case was set. Prime examples of this were the oil crisis, and the technological breakthroughs in microtechnology. In principle case instructors should not set cases when both they and their students know that the future environment will not behave in a way that was predictable at the time. To do so is to ask students to suspend belief and go through a make-believe exercise. Of course all cases are simulations and capture only some aspects of reality. But students need to believe that the situation could be real for many of the benefits of the case method to be realized. This is not possible when they know that vast changes loom just over the horizon but must be ignored in their analyses. My only advice to a student in this situation is to make the best of it. A belief in parallel universes helps!

4.1.4 Validity

Validity refers to whether the information is an accurate representation of the situation it describes. There is no necessary relationship between precision and validity. A lie can be stated in very precise terms. Indeed this is a well-known technique for making a lie believable.

It is obviously very important to establish the validity of the information in the case. Analyses or recommendations based upon invalid, or even partially valid, information are not worth much. Establishing, or at least questioning, the validity of information should be carried out at the earliest possible stage. Leaving it until later may mean wasting time and effort.

Fact or opinion?
Establishing validity is a two-stage process. In the first stage you can simply follow the clues supplied by the casewriter. The most obvious clue is whether the information is stated as fact or opinion. The following facts and opinions are fairly easy to distinguish.

Facts
'KPL had been founded by John Kennetson . . .'
'On the 1st January 1979 Noel McKinny was made managing director . . .'
'There were 93 people employed in the factory . . .'
'The four salesmen each have a territory . . .'

Opinions
'We are probably one of the few printing companies around making any sort of money'.
'They had "bought the unions off time and time again".'
'New business comes to us because of our reputation'.

Opinions are different from facts in several ways. They are situations as seen through someone else's eyes and may therefore be partial, distorted or biased. They often concern events or situations about which it would be very difficult to find out the truth. For example Alex Pendlebury claims that KPL have continually bought off the unions with resulting increases in costs and prices. This allegation would be difficult to investigate. The statement itself is not very precise. The information if available at all is probably in people's memories rather than on paper. It all happened in the past. These factors conspire to make it almost impossible to assess the validity of the statement as it was made.

Opinions are frequently concerned with relationships as well as facts. Pendlebury attributes KPL's high prices to poor trade union negotiation practices. They can be useful therefore in providing us with hints about how things work, but they are only hints. You will clearly have to regard all opinions with a degree of suspicion. It may be that you have no alternative but to treat them as valid in the absence of evidence to the contrary. However, before doing so it will be worthwhile going through a second stage of validation.

Measured how?

This second stage procedure should be applied to both facts and opinions. It consists of asking about each piece of information. 'How was that obtained or measured?' Like anyone in intelligence work you should be capable of evaluating the source of your information. Let's look at some examples.

'There were 93 people in the factory . . .'

This probably came from internal company records and there is little reason to doubt its validity.

'. . . much of its equipment was modern and efficient.'

The casewriter does not attribute this to Elwes but he is almost certainly the source. However it is probably true simply because it is not very precise. At the minimum it probably means that the factory contains a few new machines and accessories. At best it could mean that most of the equipment was new.

This raises a very general point about casewriting. In order to compress and clarify the case, casewriters may write statements which appear as facts when they are, in reality, opinions. They may be the opinions of people they have interviewed or they may be the casewriter's own. A casewriter may write 'The widget is a good, well made product.' This reads better than either 'Mr. Smith believes the product to be well made' or 'Industry opinion is that the widget is a well made product'. However, the original statement gives you no basis for assessing the validity of the statement by revealing its source. You should always beware of bold statements like this. Try to imagine where the information could have come from. Then you will be in a better position to decide how accurate it is. For example, in the Kennetson case, it is fairly obvious that the casewriter obtained all his material from company sources.

In deciding whether an opinion statement is accurate you will probably want to examine two things. First, the general credibility of the source; is the person concerned in a position where he can assess and report on situations accurately? For example, you would probably accept what Elwes had to say about the internal workings of Kennetson. But his knowledge of the print market is likely to be less accurate. You would be wise to question anything that is said on this topic which can be attributed to him.

Secondly, this examination should include not only the people quoted in the case but also the casewriter. You should be aware of what sources he may have used and how he has drawn upon them. You will soon get a feel for how a case is put together. This may allow you, in some instances, to question the validity of statements of 'fact' made in the case. You may be able to argue that the casewriter could not have known, with any certainty, what he is claiming to know. This may happen rarely but is something you should be very much aware of.

In addition to questioning individual statements, you may wish to systematically evaluate the validity of all the information that occurs in a case. It would probably be best to do this in conjunction with one of the organizing procedures, summarizing or restructuring, where the information is already listed out. An example of validity rating is given below. A numerical scale from 0 to 5 is used. A rating of 0 indicates a highly questionable piece of information. A rating of 5 suggests that there is every indication that the information is correct.

Kennetson's markets	*Validity rating*
Sales volume £2,376,000	5
Sales by category (table 1)	5
Quality end of the market	4
'New business comes to us because of our reputation'	2

Less formally you may simply wish to highlight those statements or figures which you judge to be questionable. At a minimum you should at least examine the information in the case and be aware of the main areas where validity is likely to create problems later in your analysis.

4.1.5 Extrapolating from the Information

During some of the procedures mentioned earlier in this chapter, and certainly later in the analysis, you will extrapolate from the information given. Since you may not realize the importance of this process, it will be worthwhile to examine it fairly fully now.

It is quite useful to look at the degrees of extrapolation. They are:

Facts
Inference
Speculation
Assumption

In inference you are mostly rearranging existing facts in a logical way and adding very little to them. Here are some inferences that could be made concerning the Kennetson case:

(a) Elwes is not interested in handling wage negotiations;
(b) Gaskin is frustrated and wants things to change;
(c) Pendlebury is a super salesman rather than an analytical marketing executive.

Nowhere are these statements made. However simply by collecting information together from different parts of the case you can come to these conclusions, without feeling you are making a leap in the dark.

Speculations are a mixture of facts from the case, facts imported from other sources and assumptions about how the world works. Here are some speculative statements about Kennetson:

(a) Elwes, Gaskin and Pendlebury had been at loggerheads over the last year;
(b) The unions would be prepared to discuss changes in methods of working and productivity deals at the current time;
(c) KPL is the proving ground for McKinny. If he does well he is likely to move back to a senior line post in ICAL.

Clearly the line between inference and speculation is a narrow one. The difference lies in the fact that speculation requires the importation of facts and assumptions into the case situation. The first statement (a) is really a recognition of the generalization that people of different ages and with different views and priorities will find it hard to agree on a common course of action. The second statement (b) reflects the economic view that in periods of high unemployment worker attitudes soften. The third statement (c) assumes that a common company training and assessment practice is being used in this case. These examples illustrate the fact that when you speculate you weave together facts, generalizations and assumptions. It is important to remember how the mixture was created. It is all too easy for speculation to become inference and inference to become fact as you progress with your analysis.

Assumptions
An assumption is not based upon the facts in the case. It is made because without it you cannot complete the picture or maintain a logical argument. Examples of assumptions you might make in this case are:

(a) The accounts are reasonably accurate;
(b) None of the key people are about to leave;

(c)   High unemployment will continue for at least two years;
(d)   McKinny is prepared to make sweeping changes;
(e)   The print market is highly fragmented.

Some assumptions like (a) and (c) may be so general that they apply to every case. They only become interesting in the odd situations where they don't apply. Other assumptions, for example assumption (b) are fairly specific but so unlikely to occur that they can be dismissed.

Assumptions (d) and (e) are key assumptions. There is no real evidence to support assumption (d). However without it you will be constrained in your analysis. Presumably you will wish to put yourself in McKinny's place as the decision maker. If you assume he wouldn't want to rock the boat then there is very little for you to do and the case loses its educational value. Assumption (e) is the kind of assumption you will need to make in order to carry out any kind of customer-based marketing analysis. There is no real evidence to support this in the case but without it you can't really begin to formulate a marketing strategy.

Assumptions should be visible, plausible and rare. Visible because it is easy to let assumptions creep disguised into your analysis. In particular, it is important to know and state your assumptions when discussing or writing up your analysis. Your instructor may not be happy with your assumptions, but at least he will have to credit you with the (hopefully) elegant superstructure you have built upon them. If you do not make your assumptions clear, or worse, fail to realize that you are making assumptions, your analysis will be difficult to understand and assess.

Assumptions should be plausible because otherwise it is easy to solve a problem by assuming it away. You could assume that David Elwes invented a revolutionary new printing process or that the unions will accept any demands made of them. Since you can't rely on these sorts of things happening in the real world, you shouldn't rely on them in a case analysis.

Assumptions should be rare because you must keep as close to the situation described as possible. The more assumptions you introduce the further from the original case you depart. This makes it easier to avoid rather than face the real issues involved.

4.2 GUIDE TO USE

Clearly all case analysts should heed the advice given in section 3.2 on initial reading. For the beginner, organizing the information will probably pay greater dividends than attempting to evaluate it in great detail. Since all of the organizing procedures help to familiarize you with the material in the case, it would be no great waste of effort to experiment with them all. In time you will need to develop your own style when trying to understand the case situation. Trying out these alternatives should help you to find procedures you are comfortable with.

Using systematic methods of evaluating the precision and validity of the information is probably best left to a later stage of skill development. However, you should at least read the sections dealing with these topics and be aware of the problems they create. It should be noted that information evaluations are very useful for refuting someone else's recommendations. They are also likely to impress case instructors.

Filling the gaps and extrapolating from the information given are things you will have to do anyway in any case situation. Reading the sections relating to these topics should help you to do them more effectively.

CHAPTER 5

Step Two: Diagnosing the Problems (I)

Step two is concerned with identifying problems, analyzing their nature and structure, and deciding which to tackle first.

5.1 EXAMPLE CASE—SPANLINE ENGINEERING*

George Kent was introduced to Michael Burton, the majority owner and managing director of Spanline Engineering Ltd. of Manchester, at a neighbourhood party, and their conversation drifted into a discussion of the design and layout of advertising campaigns. On learning that George was a marketing consultant and adviser to some well-known national corporations, Mr Burton asked him if he would visit his works the following week and give him an opinion on his new advertising proposals.

Michael Burton had started Spanline Engineering on a shoestring some seven years earlier when the light engineering firm for which he was works manager was taken over by a foreign producer who closed the works and replaced the manufacture with imports. Michael had been able to purchase some of the machinery at throw-out prices and hand-pick a team from the 600 men who were being laid-off. Initially he had concentrated on precision machining of light mechanical parts for machinery manufacturers on a jobbing basis, but later added a range of chain hoists of his own design. These had been very successful, with their sales growing until they now represented nearly 50% of Spanline's output.

Spanline hoists were made in three lifting capacities of 5 cwt, 10 cwt, and 1 ton, and consisted basically of a lifting block with an electrically driven sprocket that engaged the links of the lifting chain. Chain hoists of this type were officially designated as Class I cranes and appropriate for light use of up to six hours per day with continual lifts of up to 20 minutes. Heavier use would be likely to damage the hoist. Chain hoists were used widely in garages and workshops for loading machinery, and on loading docks. Mr Burton claimed that the Spanline models had no particularly outstanding features but they worked efficiently and there had been very few complaints. Although Spanline hoist blocks were larger and heavier than other makes and might last longer than the average hoist life of about five years, competitors emphasized lighter weights as a prime sales feature. Despite this, Burton felt that the larger block looked more significant and professional when installed.

The first large order for Spanline hoists came from Century Steel, a firm specializing in supplies for smaller steel fabricators and constructors. In addition to its main line of steel stocks and erection equipment, Century supplied tanks, boilers, cranes and other equipment to its customers from a network of depots throughout Britain. Century's initial order was for 500 hoists marked with their Century brand, and this had been followed with orders that grew each year then settled down to about 2,700 a year.

From time to time over the years, Michael Burton and Eric Davis, his sales director, had also called on most of the large engineering plants and engineering supply houses in the North. Orders were sporadic from these sources but totalled around 600 annually. Several large orders for Spanline hoists had also come from tenders to the Ministry of Public Works and to large industrial developments, but open invitations to bid were limited. Representatives for the various makes of cranes frequently visited purchasers before invitations to bid were issued and influenced them to limit the subsequent invitations to a few suppliers.

Two years ago Spanline had moved into a new factory built to accommodate up to 110 men, and was currently operating at about 75% of this capacity. Over the past year growth had been minimal, however, and Michael Burton and Eric Davis had finally taken a careful look at their work opportunities and decided to place more emphasis on hoist production. According to their calculations hoists were their most profitable activity. The retail prices for the 5 cwt, 10 cwt and 1 ton sizes were £180, £255 and £330 plus VAT respectively. A 17½% discount was allowed to Century Steel and most other customers and this left Spanline with an average net revenue of just over £210 per hoist, of which 55% represented materials, 20% direct labour and 25% contribution to overheads and profit. Spanline purchased castings, bearings, gears, motors, chains and electrical control gear, and then carried out the machining, assembling and finishing.

Michael Burton thought there were around a dozen crane producers in the country and knew that the Spanline production must not be enough to cover more than a small share of the national market. Compared with what he knew of the prices of competitors, moreover, Spanline's prices were among the lowest. There was thus plenty of scope for expansion, and after several long discussions Burton and Davis decided to mount an aggressive advertising campaign to extend Spanline's share of the market. Together they visited a London advertising agency, recommended to them by one of their friends,

Journal	Circulation	Frequency	Proposed Annual Insertions	Page Size of Insertions	Additional Colour	Rate £	Annual Appropriation £
Materials Handling News	20,000	Monthly	12	Full	1	492	5,904
Mechanical Handling	6,918	Monthly	6	½	—	156	936
Freight Management	20,367	Monthly	12	½	—	216	2,592
Storage & Handling Equipment News	24,972	Monthly	12	½	—	252	3,024
Industrial Equipment News	33,807	Twice Monthly	12	Full	1	744	8,928
Factory Equipment News	26,000	Twice Monthly	12	Full	—	606	7,272
							28,656

Average Monthly Readership 128,000.
Cost Efficiency = £18.9 per 1,000 readers per month.

Exhibit 5.1 Proposed Advertising Schedule

Profit and Loss Account (All entries net of VAT)	£'000	£'000
Sales		1,422
Labour	288	
Materials	660	
Work in progress variation	114	
Direct cost		1,062
Gross margin		360
Variable factory expense	171	
Fixed factory expense	57	
Selling, administrative and interest expense	48	
Directors' remuneration	33	
Total expense		309
		51
Taxation		21
Net profit		30
Balance Sheet (end of year)		
Sundry debtors	159	
Materials	75	
Work in progress	153	
Current assets		387
Bank overdraft	72	
Sundry creditors	138	
Provision for taxation	21	
Current liabilities		231
Net working capital		156
Buildings	195	
Plant and machinery	69	
Fixed assets		264
		420
Long term loan (secured)		135
Shareholders' funds		285

Exhibit 5.2 Spanline Engineering Ltd., Previous Year's Annual Accounts

which undertook to draw up a proposal for them, and Eric Davis also undertook to recruit a representative to help him on the sales side.

Most of the prospects for this sales representative post came through
leads from Davis' wide contacts in local engineering circles. He finally chose
Albert Wisdom, aged 45, who had come up from the shop floor of one of the
largest manufacturers of heavy cranes and then spent ten years in their design
office with responsibility for adapting basic crane designs to individual
customer requirements. As Davis told Michael Burton, Wisdom knew all there
was to be known about cranes. Wisdom was appointed on a good fixed salary
of £9,000 with a company car, and Mr Davis indicated that he would be
allocated a grouping of industries for which he would be solely responsible. In
this way he could build up expertise in the particular requirements of different
industries.

Eric Davis planned to retain some customer industries himself and also to
cover the customers for whom jobbing work would continue. Eric had joined
Michael Burton from the same firm when Spanline was founded and held 10%
of the shares. In his previous post he had been customer service engineer,
responsible for liaison between manufacturers and the works and had
provided many of the initial contacts for Spanline jobbing work.

When the draft proposal for the advertising scheme arrived from the
agency, Burton and Davis were impressed with the professional way in which
it was drawn up. In brief it proposed a campaign focusing on the Spanline
brand name built into a new symbol of similar shape to the hoist block. The
supporting copy emphasized the reliability and general all-purpose value of
Spanline hoists. The agency recommended that the annual appropriation be
set at £30,000 in order to make a significant impression on the market, and
that it be allocated to handling and equipment journals. They proposed the
schedule of journals set out in exhibit 5.1.

This advertising appropriation was a large sum for Spanline and Michael
Burton found himself postponing a formal letter to the agency. It was not that
Spanline lacked funds, as can be seen from the previous year's annual
accounts in exhibit 5.2, but rather Burton's unfamiliarity with advertising.
Consequently, during his conversation with George Kent about this time, he
decided to place the proposal in front of George for a second expert opinion.

*©Kenneth Simmonds 1981 (Revised). Reproduced by kind permission of the author.

5.2 PROBLEMS, OPPORTUNITIES AND THREATS

Before beginning to try to identify problems, it would obviously be worthwhile understanding what a problem is. The most useful definition for our
purposes is 'a difference between a current (or expected future) situation
and some desired situation'. Problem identification is the search for these
differences.

In the first step of the case analysis process, the existing situation has been examined and hopefully understood. In the second step you will need to compare this with the situation you might expect the organization described in the case to prefer. This comparison is dealt with in some detail in section 5.3.

First, however, a number of general points concerning problems may usefully be made now. Although the word problem is used here, problem area might be more appropriate. It is wrong to consider that there is only one problem facing an organization at any point in time—there are usually many. It is also wrong to believe that these problems are totally unrelated. They usually occur in related clusters. These clusters might more accurately be described as basic problems together with the symptoms that they generate. The complex structures of problems will be examined more closely in section 6.1.

Problems may also differ in respect of being current or future and whether they are 'good' or 'bad'. This gives a two-way classification which is illustrated in the table below.

	Present	*Future*
Good	Problems	Opportunities
Bad		Threats

Many authors like to distinguish between problems, opportunities and threats. In fact, the differences are not really all that great. The distinction between 'good' and 'bad' problems is necessary to separate opportunities from threats. This distinction has little meaning in the present. Presumably a 'good' problem would be one in which the current situation is rather better than desired. It is difficult to imagine anyone viewing that as a problem. However, in the future an opportunity is clearly a 'good' problem, as a threat is a 'bad' one. An opportunity provides an organization with the possibility of improving its performance. A threat, if it occurs, will almost certainly cause its performance to deteriorate. But both can be treated as potential problems. When an organization recognizes an opportunity, it sees a gap between what probably will occur and what could occur if it seized the opportunity. In other words the organization now has a potential problem—how to take advantage of the opportunity. In a similar fashion the organization sees the potential difference between what will happen if the threat comes to pass and if it does not. The problem is how to prevent the threat from occurring or how to minimize its effect if it does occur.

Threats and opportunities, it may also be argued, are different because they are to do with the future. But problems of any kind are also to do with the future. Obviously if a problem is only likely to be a problem now and not in the future, it ceases to be a problem. Problems derive their impact from the fact that it is believed that they will continue. In any case, you can only solve problems in the future, not in the past.

All of these arguments lead to the following conclusion. Opportunities and threats are really just special kinds of problems. You will need to be aware of their special characteristics, but in what follows the term *problems* will be used in its broadest sense to include both threats and opportunities.

5.3 LISTING PROBLEMS

The first stage in diagnosing problem areas is to list all the problems that you can identify in the case. The list for the Spanline case is given in section 5.3.5. To help you in creating this list, four sources of problems have been identified and are discussed below.

The first kind of problem is the more or less obvious one that is either pointed out to you or else is recognized from straightforward reading of the case. The second kind of problem is less obvious because it is only uncovered by using the analytical frameworks of the disciplines you are studying to evaluate the case situation. The third type of problem has to do with the future. The last results from the fact that people in organizations perceive problems in ways which differ from each other and from the case analyst.

5.3.1 Explicit Problems

The most explicit problem of all is the one you are instructed to solve. It may be that your instructor will define the problem for you. He may say 'concentrate on productivity' or 'the main problem is the attitude of the managing director'. While it is probably unwise to ignore this instruction, it is also unwise to take it too literally. Problems rarely exist in splendid isolation. They are usually related to other problems; they may even be caused by other more fundamental problems. By restricting yourself to just one problem you will usually miss the opportunity of seeing some very creative solutions. It is unlikely that your instructor will penalize you for producing better work even though you ignore the letter of his instructions.

In a similar way, do not take for granted any statement of the problem made in the case. In the Spanline case the problem is not explicitly identified but it is broadly hinted at. Burton asked Kent to 'give him an opinion on his new advertising proposals'. This may be a problem area. It is certainly not the only one; it may not even be a major one. Get used to the idea of using your own judgement to decide what problems there are in a case. Problems in real life don't come ready labelled and neatly packaged.

Problems were defined as differences between what is and what should be. So far you have become familiar with the situation in the organization in the case. In order to identify problems you now need to compare this situation with the standards that organizations use in order to discover if there are any significant differences. There are three sources of standards which you would do well to check to make sure you unearth all the problems you can.

Historic Standards

The first source of standards is history. The past is perhaps the most potent source for comparison. If things aren't as good as they used to be clearly a problem has arisen. The problem may arise in a relative or absolute form. In a commercial organization a fall in profits below last year's will usually be seen as a major problem. For a theatre company a steady decline in audience would be a major cause for concern. In both cases there has been a change in a basic measure of performance.

However, relative changes may also be important. In some organizations, used to fast growth, a slowing of that rate might be very worrying although sales, profits and other measures of performance continue to rise. It is a question of what the organization has become used to; history conditions our expectations. Conversely in some public enterprises management might feel happy to have limited the rate of increase of deficit year on year. The main underlying principle is to judge the current situation in the context of past performance. Any sharp change, either good or bad, is usually a sign that a problem exists.

For Spanline there has been one major change which has triggered off most of the activity described in the case. The sales of hoists has suddenly flattened out after growing for a number of years. This is particularly keenly felt since the company moved into a new factory only two years previously. This move was presumably made in expectation that hoist sales would continue to rise.

Environmental standards

The second source of standards comes from the environment in which the organization operates. Most frequently a comparison will be made with competing organizations. Are we as profitable as our competitors? Are we as efficient? Are we as socially responsive and responsible? The choice of peer organizations is largely a socio-political one. It may be that an organization would be quite content to simply out-perform other divisions or subsidiaries in the same group. Or it may use the whole industry or market in which it operates as a basis for comparison. A very large multi-national organization may only compare itself with organizations that operate on a similar worldwide basis.

The peer organizations need not necessarily be in the same business or carry out comparable activities. The standard for comparison may be quite remote. An organization might strive for a 'Rolls-Royce' reputation, 'Marks and Spencer' quality or the team spirit of Liverpool Football Club. In each situation the standard becomes real and important if it drives the organization to do things to meet that standard.

This is an area where external information can usefully be collected. For most types of organizations operating statistics are published and available. Indeed this type of analysis is very important to accountants. Inter-firm comparison of accounting ratios is a very powerful and frequently employed tool. The problems of comparability of accounting definitions and a need for secrecy have led to the founding of the Centre for Interfirm Comparison run under the auspices of the BIM. The Centre collects data from participating firms in the same industry and then lets an individual firm know where it lies in relationship to industry norms. This is done for an enormous variety of different ratios and the results can be displayed in the form of the pyramid of ratios described in the last chapter. As you can imagine, this is a very useful way of pin-pointing the different ways in which different firms operate and the results of doing so.

You may find that data on interfirm comparisons is included in a case study you have been asked to analyse. However, it is more likely that only the raw material, the profit and loss account and balance sheet, are provided. There are published data giving accounting ratios for different industries. If you know that the case is based on a real situation and the accounts have not been disguised, then it will be well worthwhile attempting to develop your own interfirm comparison pyramid of ratios.

You will need to be cautious on a number of counts. In an industry where every firm is badly run, the standard against which you judge the organization may not be high enough. The reverse argument applies for a very well-managed industry. Comparisons are being made with what is rather than what should be. Also you may discover that in some major areas an organization performs far worse than any competing organization. However, the organization may not regard this as important; it may not see them as relevant bases for comparison. The difference between what you think is a problem and what the organization believes is a problem will be discussed in more detail in section 5.3.4.

Spanline, at least as described in the case, seems to have few external reference points. In the bid market they are clearly unhappy that unlike their competitors they have not visited, or cannot visit, purchasers before invitations to bid are issued in order to get on the short list. Spanline hoists are heavier than those of competitors, but Burton says this is an advantage not a problem. The same remark applies to Spanline's low prices. Perhaps the major area of comparison may be in the area of advertising. Burton may well have compared his marketing operation with those of what he might regard as successful marketing companies. In doing so he may have come to the conclusion that his problem is lack of advertising. Purely on a performance level it is likely that Burton compares himself with the owners of small local engineering companies rather than the larger crane manufacturers he directly competes with. However, there is no evidence in the case to suggest that he is unhappy with overall profitability.

Control standards

A third basis for comparison stems from use of formal planning and control systems within an organization. Typically this means that an organization decides what it will achieve in a given time period, sets performance standards and compares actual performance with these standards. By definition, a problem arises when a gap (or variance) develops. In this case the standards are set by the organization. These should not, however, be taken at face value. Organizations can create problems by setting very optimistic targets. This may be used as a way of motivating employees. In this case, it is not expected that targets will be met. Conversely, if a pessimistic target is set it must not be assumed that because it is met then there is no problem. In both cases it is worth evaluating the targets independently.

In the case of Spanline there is no mention of plans or budgets and it seems unlikely that a formal planning system exists. It could not therefore have been the source of a problem. Perhaps if a formal planning system had existed the slow-down in sales might have been discovered rather earlier.

5.3.2 Implicit Problems

When you visit a doctor he will, of course, pay some attention to the symptoms you describe. However, he will then go on to make other measurements of your health. He is essentially employing a medical framework of analysis in an attempt to understand the illness you have. He is doing this in two stages. First, he measures the variables that have been demonstrated to be helpful in the diagnosis of illness (temperature, blood pressure, pulse etc.). Second, he notes which of these values are different from the measurements one would normally expect from a healthy patient. In a similar way you will have to use the frameworks of the disciplines you are learning to help you uncover organizational illness.

In chapter 3 it was suggested that you use the frameworks of the disciplines you are studying to restructure the information in the case.

The first step of this diagnosis should therefore be complete. You should have measures, albeit qualitative and imprecise, of some, if not most, of the variables that can be used to describe the dynamics of the organization. You should know what the profitability of the company is, how much it knows about its customers and how it hires people.

The next stage is to compare these 'values' with those one would normally expect from a healthy organization. In effect you will be deciding whether this organization complies with the generally accepted principles laid down for its operations. This immediately raises an enormous problem. You must be aware that the applied social sciences are not exact. There are relatively few general principles which most practitioners and theorists would agree on. There are none if you take the extreme view that principles should admit no exceptions. Some organizations can defy all the current principles of effective organizational behaviour and still succeed. Where does this leave us?

At this point in the process you are simply listing possible problems with the purpose of examining them in more detail later. It may be that what is seen as a problem at this stage will not prove to be so later in your analysis. However, it is better to include all the possible problems and then eliminate the doubtful ones later. An inclusive rather than exclusive approach may take rather more time but the resulting analysis will have fewer gaps and omissions.

The following list of possible problems was generated using marketing, accounting and management/personnel variables and is by no means exhaustive. For each problem the implication is that Spanline may have broken (or bent) some principle of organizational effectiveness. Some of the accounting problems were identified by comparing Spanline's accounting ratios to published ratios for small companies in the jobbing engineering industry.

Marketing
- (a) No real knowledge of final consumers;
- (b) Limited distribution—single distributor which in turn concentrates on small steel fabricators;
- (c) Only heavy hoist on market?
- (d) Low distributor margin;
- (e) Ineffective selling by managing and sales directors;
- (f) Lack of success in large bid market;
- (g) Lack of branding of hoists.

Accounting
- (a) Low overall profitability (4.6% return on investment);
- (b) Low profit on sales (2.1%);
- (c) Low asset productivity (2.2%);

(d)   Liquidity problems—current ratio—1.7;
                              quick ratio—0.7;
(e)   Lower contribution from hoists than jobbing.

Management/personnel
(a)   Little or no marketing expertise in the company;
(b)   Tendency to use unvetted friends and acquaintances as a source of advice;
(c)   Poor hiring practices—no job description; limited search for candidates.

From this analysis you can begin to see that the explicit problems uncovered do not tell the whole story. Spanline is in rather worse shape than it looks at first appearance. It has many of the classic problems of a small manufacturing company.

5.3.3 Future Problems

Problems are only worth considering if they are going to remain problems. It is always a useful exercise therefore to examine the list of problems you have already produced to forecast what might happen to them in the future. Did the problem result from a unique combination of circumstances which is unlikely to reoccur? Is the problem likely to continue at its current level? Is it likely to get worse, or to get better?

Spanline management really has no idea why sales growth of hoists, more specifically to Century, have stopped growing. It may simply be a temporary plateau caused by factors in the economy as a whole, in the final market for hoists or as a result of a change of policy by Century. It may, however, signal a permanent change. There is really no way of telling. In this case it is probably best to assume that the problem will continue. Even if it corrects itself the process of analysing it may create opportunities for improved performance. Conversely ignoring the problem and hoping that it will go away is a sure recipe for disaster. On examination it is apparent that most of the problems listed so far are in this category. None look as though they will solve themselves. A few look ominously as if they might get worse.

Threats and opportunities are potential future problems. They can be identified in the present but have not yet occurred and, of course, may not do so. In some case studies a threat or opportunity may be the central problem. While this is not the case with Spanline, there are some problems of this kind.

The major threat to Spanline is that Century will take its business elsewhere. This would probably bankrupt Spanline. There is no evidence concerning the relationship between Century and Spanline. It may be that hoists are neither a large nor profitable line for Century, or it may be that there are other hoist manufacturers who would be happy to supply Century on an 'own label' basis.

A second threat is that Wisdom will fail to live up to Davis' expectations. The worst situation would be if he failed to recoup his salary and overhead costs. This is a threat because the decision to employ him has been made and the outcome is not certain. Failure of the proposed advertising program would also be a threat if the decision had been made to go ahead with it. As it now stands, it remains a proposal and is therefore a current problem.

There are no obvious opportunities identified in the case. It could be argued that unutilized capacity and low penetration of both the bid and small order markets represent opportunities. However, they are already included in the list of traditional problems. Solutions to these problems would be the same thing as taking advantage of them as opportunities. An opportunity would be something like Burton having designed a radical new hoist or Spanline being offered a major export order. Nothing of this sort is evident in the case.

It is probably best not to move beyond what is in the case at this point. There are a number of suggestions that could be made about Spanline's operation. They could, for example, diversify into new products or offer themselves for sale to a major hoist producer. However, these are possible solutions to their problems and they are best left to a later stage in the case analysis process when the problems, threats and opportunities are better understood. At this stage stick to the opportunities that are specifically identified in the case material.

5.3.4 Problems for Whom?

So far the problems have all been stated in terms of the organization: Spanline has this problem or it faces that threat. But organizations are not mechanical things; they are composed of people and they operate through people. In a sense organizations don't have problems; people do. People perceive problems, are motivated to seek solutions and then are needed to implement them. In some cases people are the problem. People are the link between you, acting as the case analyst, the problems and the solutions. It is impossible to ignore the fact that you have to work with and through people. You have to do this in real life and you cannot afford to ignore it in your case analyses.

There are two main tasks you need to carry out in order to make sure that you include 'people' problems in your problem list. The first is to clarify the role you will play as the case analyst. The second is to try to determine what the people in the case perceive their problems to be.

Role clarification

Clarifying the role that a student is to take in a case analysis is an area that instructors frequently fall down on. They fail to make it clear to the student who he or she is meant to be. Clarity is of major importance here. If the student doesn't have a role the tendency is to offer vague and general recommendations. These are usually not tailored enough to the specific problem and in real life would probably be rejected as impractical. For example, what you recommend should obviously change depending on whether you are the managing director or his young graduate assistant. It is frequently difficult to get down to the nitty gritty in early case analyses. Being more precise about the role that you are taking greatly helps to prevent operating at too general a level of analysis.

If the instructor fails to make it clear which role you are to take, you should clarify the situation yourself. You may do this directly with the instructor or, if that fails, make your own choice. To help you in this, the two main possibilities are discussed below.

Firstly you may be asked, or decide, to take the role of one of the characters described in the case. In the Spanline case the obvious choice would be George Kent, the consultant. The case is written in such a way as to make the choice obvious. There is certainly one advantage in taking the role of George Kent; hardly anything is known about him except his relationship with Michael Burton. You can make what assumptions you like, within reason, about his experience, skills, attitudes and personality. You could 'play yourself' in this role and no one could argue that this contradicts the facts in the case. The more details there are in the case describing a character, the more difficult it will become for you to play that role convincingly. For example, it would be difficult for a 21-year old student to play the role of the middle-aged engineer, Burton—he does not have the background or experience. He would not be able to predict how Michael Burton would react to, say, different solutions to Spanline's problems.

In practice there is really only one answer. This is 'to put yourself in the place of' rather than 'take the role of'. You should act as if you had replaced the character concerned rather than attempting to act out his personality. You should still feel constrained by the formal work role and relationship of the position you adopt. George Kent couldn't simply assume that as a consultant he could fire Burton or Davis. A consultant, a managing director or a sales director all have rules that they must adhere to. What is suggested is that you free yourself from the restricting and very difficult task of 'acting in character'.

A second and more usual situation is to be asked to act as a consultant to the organization. 'What would you advise the organization to do under these circumstances?' Here you will be looking for more rather than less clarification. Who could a consultant sensibly be working for in this situation? You can readily make your own decisions on this issue if your instructions are not clear. If the case is given without any guidance as to your role, it is usually best to assume the consultant position. However, make sure that your assumption is explicit; this saves later misunderstandings.

Having clarified your role for yourself you can now begin to examine your relationships with the other people in the organization. In doing so you may discover even more problems. On the other hand you may solve others or realize that in your role they are insoluble and hence better left alone.

Role relationships

Individuals working for an organization will usually have a core of objectives that they hold in common. However, they may not agree on the relative importance of any single objective. In addition there will be fringe objectives about which they may fundamentally disagree. Since problems are the difference between what is being achieved and an objective or standard, it follows that individuals may not agree on what constitutes a problem. One man's problem may be another man's perfectly satisfactory situation. This is an important point. Problems motivate people to action. The gap between what is and what should be drives people to take measures designed to close that gap. If no problem is perceived, no action results. Alternatively, if a problem is seen where none exists (at least according to you as the analyst), then unnecessary actions will result. In both cases this leads to problems resulting from the perceptions that the people described in the case have of the situation in which they find themselves. You should now look at the organization and its people to see if there are any 'problem perception' problems to add to your list.

Michael Burton will not be aware of the problems already identified. This is not too important. Most of these problems are reasonably self-evident, once they are pointed out, or else they can be supported by evidence or by the results of analysis. However, he will not be very willing to admit that the following may be problem areas.

(a) Hoist too heavy? (Burton designed it)
(b) No real knowledge of final customers
(c) Ineffective selling by Burton and Davis
(d) Little or no marketing expertise
(e) Use of unvetted sources of expertise
(f) Poor hiring practices

In a sense all of these problem statements represent criticisms of the way in which the company is being managed. If any or all of these problems prove to be important, then one of the objectives of any communication of the case findings will be to present them in such a way as to convince Burton. This will usually mean a combination of collecting convincing evidence as well as couching the presentation in descriptive and objective rather than personal or critical terms.

A rather more important problem arises in the alternative situation where Burton and Davis have already decided what is wrong. Both are currently working on new promotional methods in the belief that this is the solution to their problems. They are already committed to employing Wisdom and have almost decided to advertise, the main decision being how to rather than whether to. If it is decided that this is not the best way to proceed, then Kent will have a major task in convincing Burton and Davis that they are wrong. This is particularly true since Kent is only an acquaintance and has only been asked to comment on the detail of the advertising proposal rather than the decision to promote. Clearly the situation would be rather different if you had been asked to take the place of Burton.

5.3.5 Problem Listing for Spanline

Attacking the Spanline case from a number of different directions has generated the following unordered list of some of the problems they may be facing. You should aim to produce a similar list as the first stage of diagnosing the problem in any case that you tackle.

    (a)   Lack of advertising
    (b)   What type of advertising?
    (c)   How much to spend on advertising?
    (d)   No growth
    (e)   Unused capacity
    (f)   Poor performance in bid market
    (g)   Price too low?
    (h)   Low margins to distributor
    (i)   Hoist too heavy?
    (j)   No real knowledge of final customers?
    (k)   Limited distribution
    (l)   Reliance on single distributor who may go elsewhere
    (m) Low profitability
    (n)   Ineffective selling by managing and sales director
    (o)   No branding
    (p)   Low margin on sales
    (q)   Low asset productivity
    (r)   Possible liquidity problems
    (s)   Lower contribution from hoists than jobbing
    (t)   Little or no marketing expertise in company

(u) Use of informal, unvetted sources of expertise
(v) Poor hiring practices
(w) Wisdom may fail as a salesman
(x) Burton and Davis are convinced that better promotion will solve the problem.

CHAPTER 6

Step Two: Diagnosing the Problems (II)

6.1 UNDERSTANDING PROBLEM AREAS

You now have a list of 'raw' problems. Some will be important; some will not. Some will be clear and explicit, others will be diffuse and difficult to describe. Perhaps most important of all, many of the problems will be related. It will be your task in the next stage to explore and clarify those relationships.

These relationships are important for two reasons. First, if you attempt to solve a problem without reference to other problems the organization is facing, you may get into difficulties. It may be that the problem you are concerned with can only be tackled after another related problem has been solved. For example, in the Spanline case, it would not be very sensible to tackle the problem of unused capacity without first attempting to get sales moving again. It could happen that solving one problem may make another problem worse. Putting more sales resources into the bid market might improve Spanline's sales in that area but this would probably reduce the resources available for use in the basic hoist market. These two problems cannot really be tackled if they are isolated.

There is a second, and more positive, reason for clarifying the relationships between problems. Certain problems occur as the symptoms of more basic problems. If you can identify these key problems, you may be able to solve a whole army of problems 'at a stroke'. This is not always going to be the case. However, it will at least give you an idea of which problems are more fundamental and should therefore be given priority and time.

The process of building towards a comprehensive understanding of the totality of problems facing an organization is probably best tackled in three phases. The first stage involves setting up your initial working hypotheses or models. You can do this by organizing your 'raw' list of problems into a number of different problem areas. A problem area is defined as a group of related problems. For each problem area you will then need to tentatively specify the relationships that you believe exist

60

between individual problems. The result will be a number of 'skeletons' which tentatively map out the problem areas you have identified.

The second stage is to put flesh on these 'skeletons'. To do this you will have to theorize, collect evidence, check out your theories and continue to refine and review until you are happy that you have a good understanding of each problem area.

The third stage is to prepare problem statements for each problem area. This is important not only to clarify and summarize your own thoughts but also to allow you to communicate them later when you are presenting your findings.

6.1.1 Structuring Problem Areas

Your task under this heading will be to group problems into problem areas and to try to link them. To do this you will need to understand two concepts which deal with causal relationships, i.e., relationships which describe cause and effect. The two concepts are symptoms and multi-causality.

Symptoms

Not all problems are created equal—some are more fundamental than others. Some problems cause other problems to occur. A flu virus might give rise to a headache, sore throat and aching joints. These are symptoms of the basic problem; the action of a virus. In a similar way it will be useful in organizing problem areas to distinguish between problems and symptoms. One such 'vertical' relationship from the Spanline case is tentatively mapped out in the diagram at the top of p. 62.

One way of testing a problem/symptom relationship is to ask whether the symptoms would disappear if the problem was solved. In the situation modelled in the diagram above, it is certain that resumption in growth (in real terms) would lead to a reduction in unused capacity. The problem/symptom relationship is reversible. However, there may be situations where this is not the case. A problem may result in the creation of a problem/symptom relationship which is irreversible. That is to say, removal of the problem will not result in disappearance of the symptom. For example, Spanline's creditors may learn of their liquidity problems and be unwilling to extend credit even when growth resumes. Bad personnel practices by a managing director may lead to hostile labour attitudes which would not necessarily immediately change if he were dismissed. There is an important difference here. You will usually concentrate your attention on the more fundamental problems facing an organization. You must be careful not to assume that in solving these basic problems all other problems will disappear. To remind you it is probably good practice when drawing problem diagrams to indicate

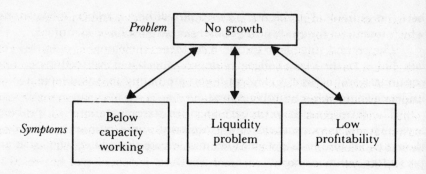

reversible relationships with a double-headed arrow and irreversible relationships with a single-headed arrow.

Symptoms can also be important in their own right. Once they are brought into existence, by more fundamental problems, they can act as barriers to the solution of other problems. Again the symptom of Spanline's liquidity problems illustrates this idea. Spanline may not have enough cash or borrowing power to buy its way out of the no-growth problem through an advertising campaign. You will usually become aware of these barriers at the evaluation stage of analysis. Nevertheless, it will be worth making a note of any symptoms that you feel may be particularly constraining on your development of alternative problem solutions. It may save you some effort if you realize early on that a whole series of solutions are ruled out because of a constraining symptom.

Multicausality

A second major concept to be aware of is that of multicausality. This simply recognizes the fact that many symptoms are caused by more than one problem. This may once again be illustrated by means of a simple problem diagram.

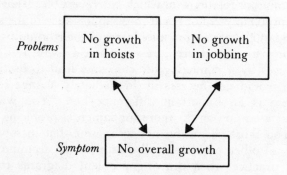

Again, it is not entirely clear that these relationships are correct. It can be inferred that most of the growth in the past has been due to hoists and it has been their sudden levelling out which has created the no-growth problem. Note that this situation would have been rather different if hoist growth had just offset the decline in jobbing. The emphasis might then have been on the problems of the jobbing market rather than those of the hoist market.

Multicausality introduces horizontal relationships into the structuring of problems. It forces you to face the complexity of problem areas as they appear in case descriptions. Multicausality has another unfortunate side effect. If two problems help to produce the one symptom then removal of one of the problems may not lead to the disappearance of that symptom. In the illustration above this is happily not the case. A return to increasing hoist sales would lead to a return to overall company growth assuming that jobbing sales remained the same. However, consider the following situation.

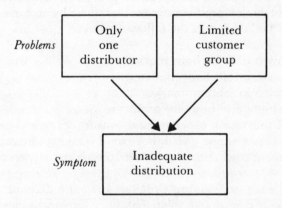

Here it is argued that inadequate distribution is caused by having only one distributor and by the fact that that distributor has a limited customer group. Adding more distributors would only help if they extended the customer group. Another Century would probably do little to improve distribution. Conversely, convincing Century to sell to a wider customer group would not necessarily solve the distribution problem. There is a limit to what one distributor can do. In summary it really seems that both problems must be tackled before the symptom will disappear. The complex relationship between problems and symptoms that multicausality leads to means that you cannot always expect to solve one problem and then watch everything else drop into place. On the other hand, it does mean that you are unlikely to offer simplistic and naive single cause solutions to complex organizational problems.

Problem diagrams

Having understood the twin concepts of symptoms and multicausality you are now ready to work on your list of raw problems. Your objective is to draw up problem diagrams which are your preliminary ideas or hypotheses of the problem areas and their structures. The type of system diagrams used in the illustrations in this section are well suited to the structuring of problem areas. Verbal descriptions usually lack clarity and are difficult to manipulate. Mathematical descriptions of problems are rarely possible in case studies. Systems diagrams represent a useful middle ground.

You may begin by simply grouping together those problems which seem to you to be related. An alternative approach is to pick out what you believe the fundamental problems to be and then to fit the other problems/symptoms around them. You should attempt to fit in all your problems somewhere.

Figure 6.1 is a problem diagram which incorporates most of Spanline's problems as listed in section 5.3.5. These problems have been grouped into a number of major problem areas, identified by the use of dotted lines. These can be labelled in the following way:

(a)   no growth in basic hoist market
(b)   no growth in bid hoist market
(c)   no growth in jobbing market
(d)   profitability and liquidity problems
(e)   lack of marketing expertise and consumer knowledge
(f)   threat that a single distributor could bankrupt Spanline
(g)   premature conviction that advertising is the answer.

Some problems were excluded in order to keep the diagram relatively simple. Others were considered isolated and less important. For example, poor hiring practices have not been included for these reasons. Isolated problems usually tend to be either relatively trivial or else problems which there is very little information about. 'No growth in the jobbing market' comes into the latter category. It is obviously an important area but there is very little information in the case concerning it.

Note that the major problem areas are almost all linked together. In some cases the linkage is so close that the separation appears somewhat arbitrary. This is not very important. The boundaries can always be redrawn in the next stage when the relationships are examined in more detail. Where the links are relatively remote the problems can be treated separately.

It must be emphasized that this is a preliminary sketch. Many of the links are tentative. In some cases it is felt that other factors may influence a problem but that these have not been identified yet. This is indicated by

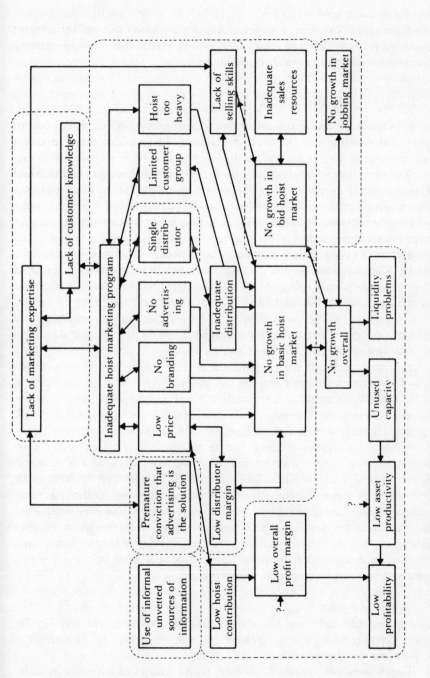

Figure 6.1 Spanline Engineering Ltd., Problem Diagram for Some of the Problem Areas

a question mark and an arrow. Nevertheless, diagrams like this form a basis from which to work; a series of hypotheses to check out. In the next section ways in which you can develop and refine this model—putting flesh on the bare bones—will be discussed.

6.1.2 Developing Problem Areas

The problem area diagrams are essentially frameworks which attempt to capture the problems facing an organization. The next step is to develop those structures; to test and refine the hypotheses you have proposed. The output of this stage of analysis will be the best definitions you can make of the problems as you see them. They will form the basis of your subsequent analysis and therefore require careful thought and a lot of work.

Developing your problem model is best viewed as a cyclical process comprising three different activities—testing, restructuring and elaboration. Testing means checking the structure you have proposed for each problem area to see if it is consistent with the available evidence. If either a problem or a relationship between problems looks suspect, then you might decide to restructure. Finally when you are happy that the overall structure works you will want to look at certain key problems and relationships in order to map them out in more detail. At any stage you may decide to go back or forward to another stage in the process. Looking at a problem in detail may suggest a new structure which then needs testing. Testing a relationship might reveal some interesting ways in which it could be made more detailed. Each activity depends on and is related to the others. The important point is to keep your eye on the goal: detailed, logically structured, well researched definitions of the problems.

All three activities require you to do further research and collect more information. The information can come from a number of different sources. These have already been identified in chapter 3. It may be worthwhile to remind yourself what these sources are and their main characteristics. Using information in this context is however somewhat different from the way in which you will have used it earlier in your analysis. Now you are concerned with specific relationships. You should therefore be in a position to define fairly precisely what information you require. This in turn makes it easier to find.

Testing and restructuring

Testing and restructuring are closely linked activities and will be discussed together using the price/no growth relationships as illustrated in the problem diagram below.

There are two aspects of any relationship which you will be interested in—strength and direction. At one extreme the strength of a relationship may be zero, i.e., there is no relationship between the two

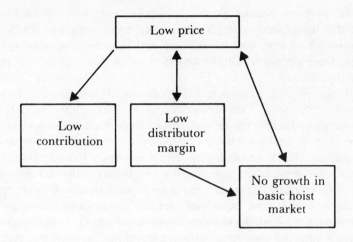

problems. At the other extreme one problem may be the single, unequivocal cause of a particular symptom. Some relationships exist by definition. For example, if there is no growth in any of Spanline's markets, then there must be no growth overall.

When a problem, like no growth in the basic hoist market, has a number of possible causes, then it is obviously of great importance to estimate the relative strength of each. Only in this way can you concentrate your efforts on solving the key rather than subsidiary problems. In this situation is price as important as advertising or distribution?

The direction of the relationship may also be important. It has already been pointed out that because a problem has created a symptom, this does not mean that when the problem has been solved the symptom will also disappear. In this case, for example, a higher price might mean a higher distributor margin but no change in the low contribution that Spanline receives. Every relationship should be examined to see whether it is reversible or not.

Causality need not run in just one direction. In some cases it may be impossible to discover in which direction it flows. For example, the relationship between inadequate selling resources and the small share of the bid market could be argued either way. Low selling effort could have led to low sales. However, a history of low sales could have convinced Burton and Davis that the market was too difficult to compete in and therefore that they should devote little selling effort to it. In this kind of situation you are left with little choice but to try to predict what would happen to the second problem if you solved the first.

An example
Let us examine the example to see how the various relationships might be

tested and perhaps restructured. Remember you are not looking for evidence that a problem exists. You have already satisfied yourself earlier that it does. You are now concerned with the relationships between problems. Does problem A have an effect on problem B, and if so how strong is that effect?

Looking first at the low price/no growth relationship the question is, 'what evidence is there that low price can restrict sales growth?'. This may be particularly difficult to understand since Burton has said that the Spanline hoist is heavier and looks 'more significant and professional when installed'. In this case it is possible to bring in information from outside the case. One of the principles of marketing is that all the various parts of a marketing program should be consistent. A high quality product selling at a low price delivers an inconsistent message to a potential customer. Perhaps the slowdown in sales means that Spanline is reaching the limit of the 'price above everything' segment of the hoist market. There is therefore some evidence to suggest that low price may be a problem affecting the sales of hoists. This is reinforced by the other factors also thought to affect hoist sales. A low price might not matter for a product if it was branded (and hence made reputable) and the reason for the low price used as the basis for a promotional campaign. The three factors—low price, no branding and no advertising might well be a particularly potent combination in stunting sales growth. While this idea requires no restructuring of the problem diagram, nevertheless, the three factors may be grouped together to remind us that they should perhaps be treated as an interacting group.

The relationships between low price and low contribution/low distributor margin must be examined together. It is logically true that the final price to the customer is simply the sum of the distributors margin and the price charged by Spanline. The price charged by Spanline in turn determines the contribution to overheads and profit that hoists make. Thus, any price increase or decrease has to be allocated between Spanline and Century. The relationships are straightforward accounting ones although the effect that they can have on other problems is not. A low margin for Century simply means they are not going to exert much effort for an inadequate return. Indeed the whole area of Century's reasons for handling Spanline's hoists is a candidate for more detailed analysis. Perhaps they are attempting to establish a whole line of 'own label' products. It may be that they require hoists to complete their line and don't expect them to generate either much volume or profit. It may be possible to get information outside the case which would help to throw some light on the situation. In the end, though, the key question is, 'Does the low margin to Century inhibit its effort on Spanline's behalf?'. Equally important is the corollary, 'Would increased margins motivate them to sell more?'. Century sells 'steel stock, erection equipment, tanks, boilers, cranes and other equipment to its customers from a network of depots throughout Britain'. Most of this is high volume, high price material. It may be that 2700 hoists at £70 each is not a major item for them. The addition of a few percentage points on the margin may not have too much effect. The relationship between low margin and low growth may therefore be called into question. Nevertheless, it could be important if Spanline decided to use distributors other than Spanline. The problem diagram may therefore need some restructuring and might now look something like this.

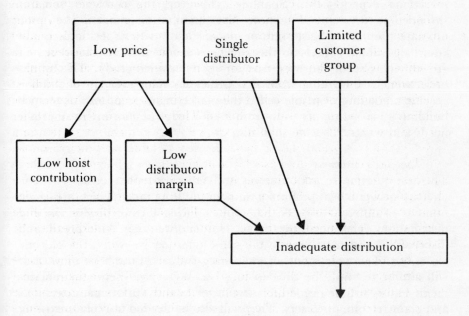

Low distributor margins are now acting with the other distribution factors to create a rather complex distribution problem.

This is an example of how problem diagrams are developed. The evidence in favour, and against, a relationship is collected and weighed and a judgement is made. New structures and relationships may be seen and substituted for old ones. The process is an iterative one ending usually when evidence finally runs out or when the assumptions you are forced to make become too implausible.

Elaboration

In the previous example it became clear that the relationship between Century and Spanline was rather more complex than the problem diagram indicated. This relationship needs breaking down into a number of subproblems and relationships before it can be fully understood. In other words, this part of the problem diagram needs elaborating; it needs to be modelled in more detail. However, it seems obvious even this early in the analysis that Century will not remain the only distributor for long. It simply represents too much of a risk to continue a single distributor policy. We should perhaps turn to another and potentially more important area of the problem diagram.

The key causes of the inadequate marketing program are given as inadequate marketing expertise and inadequate customer knowledge. We are probably quite clear about the origins and nature of the lack of hoist marketing experience in Spanline. However, the customer remains shrouded in mystery. We know that Spanline is ignorant about the ultimate user of its hoists but we do not know what specific pieces of knowledge are likely to be the key ones involved in its slowdown in growth. This seems an area ripe for more detailed study. This would have been true working from first principles. However, in addition a specific marketing principle called the marketing concept tells us to start building a marketing program from a knowledge of consumers and their needs and wants. This we shall now do.

Spanline's customers

The first question to ask ourselves is, 'Why do people buy hoists?' The obvious answer is—to perform a number of lifting tasks. There are a vast number of different objects that require lifting during production and distribution. The need for hoists is therefore very widespread and dispersed. Another answer to the same question is—when the old one wears out. This points out an interesting feature of the hoist market. It will almost certainly be divided into two segments—new and replacement. Hoists will be needed for new factories and workshops, extensions and plant retooling projects. They will also be needed to replace existing hoists. The nature of the two markets are likely to be rather different. Their basic differences are noted in the table below.

	New market	Replacement market
Customers/deciders	Architects	Purchasing managers
	Project managers	Production managers
	Top management	Foreman
Requirements	Highly specified	Quick replacement
	Bulk discount	Price almost immaterial
Characteristics	Concentrated	Dispersed
	Expert buyers	Loyal buyers
	Highly scrutinized	Little thought/concern
	Large orders	Small orders

From this analysis it can be seen that while Spanline may not be catering to the needs of the replacement market very well, it is hardly touching the new market at all. Century will on the whole not be involved in the new market except peripherally—it would require too much specialized effort on their part. They are mainly concerned, as most industrial distributors are, with high volume, repeat-order material like steel and the straightforward replacement of standard equipment like hoists, boilers and erection equipment.

It is difficult to avoid the conclusion that Spanline has reached the current sales plateau because they have reached a saturation sales level with Century in the replacement market of that company's limited range of customers. If we were happy with this diagnosis, the problem diagram might be restructured and elaborated to look like this.

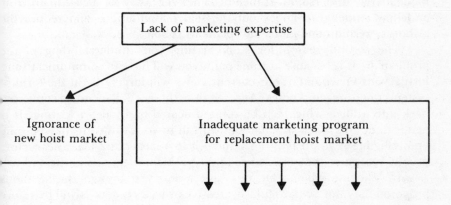

Based on our customer analysis it would be easier to determine not only the relative strength of the various pricing, distribution and promotion problems we have already identified, but also how they arise. For example, we have deduced that price is not particularly important in the replacement market because the amount involved for any one purchase is not large. Spanline's low price, far from being a positive advantage, is likely to signal low quality to a buyer.

This process of detailing and elaboration must be carried out with judgement. It obviously will not pay to examine each problem or relationship in the same detail. Here the problem diagram is a great help. It enables you to see at one time the overall structure of a problem area and hence to concentrate your attention on the crucial areas.

The output from this stage of the diagnosis will be a fairly elaborate systems diagram of the major problem areas. The next stage is to codify this knowledge by means of succinct problem statements.

6.1.3 Stating the Problems

You have reached the end of a long and somewhat complex process at this point. It is now time to take stock and summarize your position. This serves two purposes. First, it will help you to clear up any inconsistencies and errors that may have crept into your analysis of the problem areas you have uncovered. By stating the problems in another way, you will have a chance to review and improve on your understanding. The whole of the rest of the analysis you do will be based upon the problem areas as you have described them. It is hardly an exaggeration to say that completing the definition of the problem takes you more than half way through the total analytical process. It pays to make sure that the problems are defined as accurately as possible. Students frequently make the mistake of rushing on and attempting to solve problems they have inadequately understood. It then becomes very easy for a case instructor or fellow student, to knock out the shaky foundations and reduce the elaborate recommendations and plans to rubble.

The second reason for summarizing your understanding of the problem areas is because at some point you will have to communicate and justify your viewpoint. Your current views will largely be in the form of systems diagrams and notes. At some time these will have to be converted back into a form which can be communicated orally or in writing. It is better to do this when the material is fresh in your mind. It may become unintelligible if you leave transcribing it to a later date! Case instructors usually recognize the importance of the problem diagnosis phase and will reward students who tackle this task well, even though the solutions proposed may not be particularly creative or well chosen. It will therefore pay you to spend time polishing problem statements. Discussions of problem areas also occur early in case sessions. The student who can briefly and cogently outline the key problem areas, and the evidence which supports these views, will stand out. Later in the session discussion usually becomes more ragged and it is more difficult to get over a closely argued and complicated viewpoint.

Problem statements

Problem area statements will usually be verbal. This is the form of communication which works best in a case discussion or an oral presentation. For a written presentation systems diagrams or even mathematical equations can be used, but these are better used sparingly. Problem area statements should be as concise as possible—they should point out the gaps that have created the problems and symptoms. They should also broadly indicate the relationships among problems within a problem area. Problem statements should, as far as possible, avoid implying solutions. Sometimes this will be impossible. In general, though, you will want to leave room for a number of alternative solutions to be considered.

Below is a problem statement for the 'no growth in basic hoist markets' problem area in the Spanline case.

Problem Statement

Spanline Engineering—'No growth in basic hoist market' problem area

Hoist sales to small scale customers, mainly through Century Steel, have suddenly levelled out after several years of rapid growth. This was caused by an inadequate marketing program in turn resulting from lack of marketing expertise in this kind of market coupled with, and partly causing, an inadequate knowledge of consumers. The marketing program fails most significantly in the area of distribution —one distributor with a limited customer group working on a low margin. This gives poor coverage of a limited proportion of the replacement market and almost no coverage of the new market. Spanline has no brand image, does no advertising and has little in the way of selling skills. It is also possible that the design of the hoist may be contributing to the overall sales stagnation. The low price contradicts the quality brand image that Spanline seems to want to project. The marketing program is inconsistent, unplanned and not based upon an understanding of consumer behaviour.

In addition to making a problem statement you might wish to list the evidence in support of the statement. This can be in the form of short notes simply to remind you why you have said what you have said. For the example above the notes might look, in part, like this.

(a) 'Over the past year growth has been minimal' (probably means sales but could mean profits, too)
(b) Burton and Davis galvanized into action by the slowdown so they see it as important
(c) Century sales are 80% of basic hoist sales
(d) Century sells to 'smaller steel fabricators and constructors'
(e) Typical margin for equipment is 20–25%
(f) Burton and Davis had 'called on most of the large engineering plants and supply houses'. 'Orders were sporadic . . .'
(g) Burton is a former works manager; Davis was a customer service engineer on the jobbing side of the business.

A problem statement should be completed for all of the problem areas you have identified. In the next stage you will need to begin to choose among these problem areas and decide which should have prior attention.

6.2 CHOOSING PROBLEM AREAS

You will usually manage, in most case studies, to identify a relatively large number of problem areas. The next problem is to choose which to attempt to solve. You will have limited time and resources and you will obviously wish to use them to the best advantage.

The first point that should be made is that you should tackle only one problem area at a time. In theory this could lead you into difficulties—problem areas are related, and it could be that a piecemeal approach could lead you to solutions which make other problems worse. Nevertheless, it is almost impossible in even the simplest case to keep all of the balls in the air at once. Solving all the problem areas simultaneously is just too difficult an intellectual problem. The best compromise is to treat them sequentially and then go through the whole array of solutions making sure that they are consistent. This will be touched upon later in the evaluation stages of the case analysis process.

Given that problem areas are to be tackled one by one it is necessary to have some means of establishing priority among them. Five criteria have been developed which should help you in your decision:

Priority criteria
(a)   The first criterion is that of importance to the organization. In other words, which problem area creates most threat to the organization in its pursuit of organizational goals. The ultimate threat would of course be extinction. Any problem area which threatens the survival of the organization is clearly going to require early attention. Most cases involve less dramatic situations than this. Nevertheless, it is usually possible to distinguish between problems that are likely to have different effects on an organization's growth, activity, profits or other measure of organizational achievement. Obviously the more important the problem area, the higher its priority.
(b)   A second criterion is that of urgency. A major problem which can only be tackled in the long term might take second place to a problem that requires your attention now. It is important to attempt to judge the time scale of problems. One way to do this is to decide what is the last moment you could leave the problem to before it became insoluble, or created an irreversible situation that you would prefer did not occur. The nearer the deadline, the more urgent the problem. Again it is obvious that, other things being equal, urgent problems should be attempted first.
(c)   The third criterion has less to do with the problem, more to do with the solution. In general it is probably wise to start with the

easiest problems; problems which look as though they will be relatively easy to solve. Apart from the obvious psychological boost of working quickly through the easiest problems, there is also a theoretical reason for this principle. Easy problems usually have a number of solutions. If the more difficult problems are tackled later and if there is a conflict or inconsistency between the solutions to the difficult and easy problems, then alternative solutions to the easy problems can be substituted. At the extreme, insoluble problems should be eliminated altogether. These will usually be problems over which the organization, or the case analyst, has little or no control. They should be noted and then ignored.

(d)   Some problem areas are more central than others. The fourth criterion has to do with this quality. It is really a matter of productivity. Problem areas tend to be linked to a greater or lesser extent. If you can solve a problem which casts its shadow over a number of other problem areas, then this is a highly productive move.

(e)   Finally, there is an educational criterion. The first four criteria ignore the fact that case studies are educational experiences with educational objectives. This must be reflected in your choice of problem area priorities. Case instructors may set cases in order for you to employ particular techniques or concepts, or else to examine a particular aspect of organizational life in some detail. This may lead you to ignore the important, urgent, central problems in favour of problems which allow you to practise particular skills. For example if a marketing instructor set the Spanline case he would not be very happy if you concentrated on management structure and practice problems even if you could demonstrate that they were more important than the marketing problems. However, it is also acceptable in my view that you should concentrate your attention on problem areas which allow you to practise the skills you wish to learn rather than those your instructor would prefer you to learn.

The most important, urgent, easiest, central and educationally desirable problem area is the problem to start with. However, as usually happens in these cases, the most important problem may be the most difficult. The most central problem is the least educationally desirable. A compromise is called for; trade-offs must be made.

6.3 GUIDE TO USE

All case analysts, whether experienced or beginners, will probably gain something from reading section 5.2 on understanding the nature of problems, opportunities and threats. The beginning case analyst will probably wish to keep to a simple problem listing (section 5.3.5) and then choosing among these problems using the ideas discussed in section 6.2.

The next stage of development will involve moving from a simple problem listing to problem structuring (6.1.1) and problem area development (6.1.2) before summarizing the analysis done at this stage through problem statements (6.1.3).

CHAPTER 7

Step Three: Creating Alternative Solutions

Step three begins with the creation of alternative solutions to the problems identified in step two. These need to be combined and organized so that choosing among solutions can be carried out efficiently, in a series of stages.

7.1 EXAMPLE CASE—TRAIDCRAFT LTD.

In early December 1980, Richard Adams, Director of Traidcraft Ltd., was looking forward to a very busy pre-Christmas rush. Traidcraft staff were already beginning to work Saturday mornings on the fifth floor of the warehouse in Carliol Square, Newcastle, from which Traidcraft operated. Richard Adams had this to say about the problems facing him.

> "Above all we need product to sell. Already we are out of stock on a number of items with little chance of delivery before Christmas. This is a long-term problem too. Our suppliers are Third World cottage industries. There aren't many producing the kinds of products that we can sell in a developed economy or that can cope with trading to developed country standards. On top of that there is the problem of unearthing them.
>
> We have cashflow problems and so do our suppliers. On the one hand we prefer to give producer groups large and regular orders so that they can plan efficiently and so we can give guaranteed delivery to our customers. This means we hold high stocks but can't really ask for extended credit from suppliers. In some cases this would mean they couldn't afford to buy raw materials. One shouldn't grumble, though. These are the problems of success and there is little enough of that about at the moment."

Traidcraft Ltd. officially began trading on 1st August 1979 after about six weeks of intensive preparation. Four weeks later the first, monochrome mail order catalogue went out as the first deliveries from producer groups began arriving. In the first (eight-month) financial year to March 1980 sales were £124,000 and profits £12,000. The budget for 1980/81 called for sales of £256,000 and a net surplus of £30,000. Sales to November 1980 were £15,000 above budget.

Traidcraft was formed to market Third World products in the UK. It is a Christian direct-action organization dedicated to help correct the imbalance of wealth between developed and less developed countries. Its main strategy is to help develop small scale, local craft industries by acting as a marketing agency for their goods. As a general policy Traidcraft acts on strictly commercial lines, paying the market rate to producers and selling at competitive prices in the UK. Trade rather than aid is the aim. Only by acting commercially can Traidcraft ensure that producers will be able to compete on equal terms in world trade markets. Traidcraft aims to make a net 10% overall profit on sales to finance its own expansion and growth.

Traidcraft's current product range mostly comprises craft products made from jute, straw, cane, wood and cloth. They are usually decorative rather than functional, small and light for easy distribution, and retail for less than £5. Traidcraft receive a trickle of sample products from producer groups for possible inclusion in their product line. Recent possibilities include coffee beans from Tanzania and expensive traditional carpets woven by Tibetan refugees in North India. Producer groups learn of Traidcraft through the many aid and voluntary organizations that exist to help Third World countries to industrialize. Currently the products are evaluated by Richard Adams and his staff, and no formal market research is carried out to test consumer reactions.

Traidcraft has, in its short life, bought from over 30 producer groups in seven countries. In general Traidcraft require the producer groups they deal with to be organized for the benefit of their members and to be making, or have the potential to make, commercially viable products. Traidcraft directors normally visit producer groups before they agree to take their products and may offer advice and assistance.

There are three main channels through which Traidcraft sells and distributes its products—Voluntary Representatives, mail order and wholesaling to conventional retail outlets. The percentage of sales through each of these channels were budgeted to be 35%, 25% and 40% respectively for the financial year 1980/81. Currently both mail order and Voluntary Representatives sales are way above budget but wholesale sales are very much below.

Traidcraft currently has over 300 Voluntary Representatives with applications running at 8–10 per week. They sell through craft parties, stalls at bazaars, fetes and markets and even door-to-door selling. Most Voluntary Representatives are attached to churches and Traidcraft would prefer that selling and education about the Third World go hand in hand. Voluntary Representatives receive up to 25% discount off catalogue prices depending on the value of their order. They may keep this commission or donate it to a charity. Voluntary Representatives distribute the mail order catalogue to prospective buyers and use it to sell from. Traidcraft prefer but do not insist that their Voluntary Representatives are Christians. The average annual sales per representative are about £500.

The first monochrome mail order catalogue was something of a disappointment. Sales hardly covered costs. However, the second colour catalogue has been very much more successful after its introduction in September 1980. Catalogues are distributed by Voluntary Representatives and to callers at Carliol Square. In addition a direct mail shot is sent via a mailing list that Traidcraft is developing. A small number of newspaper advertisements with reply coupons are also used. Catalogues cost 60p each to produce and 25,000 were printed. Average orders by mail are around £18.

Traidcraft has over 500 wholesale accounts mainly with small craft shops but including Heals, Rackhams, Fenwicks and some other major department and chain stores. The wholesale price list offers discounts from 35% to 50% off mail order prices depending on the quantities ordered. The majority of the accounts were obtained at trade fairs in Olympia, Torquay and Birmingham, although 4,000 gift shops were mailed a trade catalogue and three commercial agents were retained on a commission-only basis. Traidcraft believe that their wholesale activities are very important since they act as a test of the long-term commercial viability of their products.

7.2 PROBLEMS AND SOLUTIONS

Developing solutions will be tackled in a similar way to that used for identifying problems. First a bank of possible solutions will be developed and then this will be organized and combined in much the same way that problem areas were created.

This method of producing solutions relies on two principles governing creativity. After all, this is the key creative process in the whole of your analysis. Firstly, all other things being equal, the more solutions produced the better the final choice is likely to be. There must of course be limits to this process. Too many solutions make the task of judging them very difficult. Nevertheless it is probably best to have an embarrassment of riches rather than the reverse. The second principle is that you should postpone judgement of newly created ideas. Creative thought leapfrogs: one idea leads to another. Killing an idea at birth, because it seems at first glance impractical, may close a potentially fruitful line of thought.

All of this suggests that the problem, rather than the problem area, should be used as the basic unit of operation. If you try to develop a consistent set of solutions for a whole problem area, you will inhibit creativity. The need to be consistent will exclude many, perhaps very interesting, solutions to individual problems. What is more, solutions for one problem may suggest other solutions for other problems. The process must be kept freewheeling and free from constraint.

Importance of creativity

The importance of creativity in this step of the case analysis can hardly be over-emphasized. Students of the case method usually perform this task rather badly. It is not that students using the case method are inherently less creative than students using other learning experiences, it is more an attitudinal problem. Case instructors and texts usually stress the logical nature of case work. Cases are said to be about logical problem solving; creating order out of chaos. This is true but it is only half of the story. Problem solving requires creativity too. In many ways the results of creative work tend to be more important than the results of logical thought. Ask a manager which he would rather have, a beautifully described problem with no hint as to how it might be solved or a creative solution to an ill-defined problem. Most would see the value of the former while choosing the latter.

It is quite commonplace to find that case students propose rather pedestrian solutions to the pressing problems facing an organization. However, there is a relatively straightforward way around this. First it has been shown that if people are specifically told to be creative, then their creative productivity increases enormously. It seems that some kind of permission is required before people will allow themselves to indulge in flights of fancy. I am doing more than giving you permission; I am urging you to be creative. I have no doubt you will find it an exhilarating process. You will also find that your case analyses will benefit from a dose of 'blue sky' thinking.

A second point is that creativity can be improved by the use of creativity techniques. These techniques will be discussed in some detail in section 7.3.3. Sitting down in front of a blank sheet of paper can be daunting. A few simple but productive hints are all that is required to get over any creative block that you may experience.

Relationship of problems to solutions

Problems and solutions do not necessarily have a one-to-one relationship. In generating solutions you should be aware of this because it should influence the way in which you create and define your solutions. There are three possible relationships between problems and solutions and these are best described in terms of a simple diagram (figure 7.1).

In situation 1 the solution fits the problem exactly. That does not necessarily mean that it is the best or even a good solution. What it means is that the solution is only concerned with that problem. In the Traidcraft case, for example, increasing the wholesale discount may or may not increase sales through this channel. However, this solution is addressed

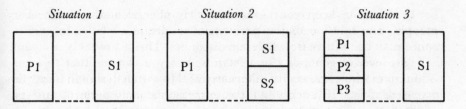

Figure 7.1 Problems and Solutions

solely to the problem of 'disappointing sales in the wholesale sector' and to no other.

The second situation is perhaps more common. A solution may prove to be only a partial solution. In this case it becomes necessary to add another solution to the original in order to fully encompass the problem. You should be aware when you are proposing only partial solutions. It is probably best to form a compound solution immediately; otherwise you may forget that you have left half of the problem hanging in mid-air. Again, Traidcraft provides an example. Traidcraft has a cashflow problem: A traditional way to improve cash flow is to squeeze debtors. In this case it would mean giving less credit to customers. However, there is a limit to which this can be done without affecting sales. On the other side of the cashflow equation suppliers are in no better position to offer Traidcraft long credit lines. The problem has to be tackled from both directions at once.

In the third situation one solution may encompass a number of different problems. Forming a Third World importing company in conjunction with Oxfam, Tearcraft, FRIDA and any other interested bodies would fall into this category. In this case it is wise to include the solution under the headings of all the problems it might help to solve. Broad-ranging solutions may have another characteristic: they may not only offer solutions to several problems but may also reveal new opportunities. In the example given above the buying power of the group might be sufficient so that they could set up producer groups to make products to specific designs rather than simply supporting groups already making a given range of products.

General solutions

This leads to a more general point. Problems have been identified and need to be solved. They should therefore be the starting point when looking for solutions. They should not constrain you from looking beyond to, perhaps, defining new problems or hopefully new opportunities. What you recommend will be judged on how far forward it pushes the organization towards achieving its goals; this may move far beyond simply solving today's problems.

It is best to keep your solutions fairly general at this stage. For example, one solution to the problem of inadequate wholesale performance may be to increase wholesale discounts. This is probably at about the right level of generality as it stands, but you can see that this has within it a whole galaxy of alternatives. How much should they be increased? 5%? 10%? Should the increase be across the board or weighted towards high volume or low volume purchases? Should the discount system be applied to single orders or to all orders over a period of time?

Restricting solutions to a general nature makes the process of organizing them easier. It both reduces the number to be dealt with and it clarifies the main alternatives. Having decided that, at a general level, one alternative is better than another, it then becomes relatively straightforward to decide how that alternative is to be implemented at the level of detail. This top-down approach will be discussed further in section 7.4. For now the advice is not to get involved in detail but to try to see the broad problem–solution picture.

7.3 SOURCES FOR SOLUTIONS

7.3.1 Experience and Knowledge

One of the most frequently used sources of inspiration for problem solutions is experience. Having faced similar problems in the past we are often apt to try again the solutions which worked then. This does not imply that you must have extensive organizational experience. We all meet problems in our day-to-day existence with other individuals, groups or institutions. We have a rich background of experience to draw on simply from our knowledge of day-to-day life.

A second source of ideas is knowledge of how other people tackle their problems. Again, we normally have a vast store of second-hand knowledge which can prove to be a treasure trove of possible solutions. In addition, if imagination fails, it is always possible to specifically seek out information about people or organizations facing problems similar to those you are now facing.

In your development of solutions, experience and knowledge will be only one source of inspiration. There should be little need to emphasize that experience and other people's solutions may not be a good guide to action. Organizational decision-making is frequently hidebound by what has worked in the past. In case study situations you can afford to break free from convention and broaden your problem-solving horizons.

7.3.2 Academic Disciplines

As mentioned a number of times earlier, it is unlikely that you will be using case studies in a vacuum. You will normally be using them after, or in parallel with, a course based on an academic discipline such as management, social administration or education. In general it is the applied social sciences like these that make use of case studies as training grounds. The applied nature of these disciplines means that they have developed a body of normative principles, strategies and tactics which have proved useful or successful in situations which form their focus of study. These principles, strategies and tactics will therefore form a bank of possible solutions from which you may choose.

For example, in marketing there are the strategies of market segmentation, market penetration, market development, product development and diversification. In purchasing you might think about vendor rating schemes, multiple sourcing, materials management and value analysis. As a student of production you would wish to see Gantt charts, Critical Path Analysis, line of balance and linear programming work. You will know what are the relevant principles in your own discipline and will need to search among them for any that are applicable.

In many ways your basic discipline should be your first and most important source of solutions. After all, you should not have to reinvent the wheel each time you face a problem. Other minds have developed powerful strategies. It seems inefficient not to consider them. It will also be more appealing to your instructor if you can show that you have at least considered the possibility that what you have been taught has real life application.

Again a word of caution. It has already been pointed out that cases have no single analytical solution. The strategy you may decide to include as one possible solution will usually be couched in very general terms. You will have to do a certain amount of bridge building before you can convert it into a specific and usable solution.

For example, multiple sourcing might seem an excellent strategy for Traidcraft. In effect it would protect its suppliers by getting the same goods from more than one producer group. However, this strategy takes you only a small part of the way. Do you rely on chance to discover two sources of the same products? Would Traidcraft need to set up alternative producer groups? Would the groups cooperate and coordinate their activities even if they were on different continents? As you can see, a lot more detailed creative works needs to be done before this can be turned into a practical proposition.

Again it should be emphasized that this is only one source of possible solutions. Too great a concentration on discipline-based solutions may help your understanding of the subject but it will restrict the skills you learn. No applied social science is yet at the stage where case studies become merely exercises in applying principles.

7.3.3 Creativity Techniques

Perhaps the most venerable of all creativity techniques is *brainstorming*. This presents something of a problem to the case analyst since they are essentially group techniques. Of course it may be that you will be working in a group, in which case brainstorming techniques are particularly appropriate for one session during the preparation of a group presentation.

The basic principles of brainstorming have been encapsulated as 'Postpone judgement, freewheel, hitch-hike, quantity breeds quality'. These can be interpreted in the following practical way. Write every idea down, no matter how stupid or irrelevant it seems. Relax and let ideas come rather than trying to concentrate on logical progressions of thought. Use your list of ideas to generate new ideas. Keep on even though your list is long and productivity seems to be flagging. This is the first stage of the brainstorming technique. The second stage involves evaluating the list of ideas you have generated, one for each problem. Many will be immediately discarded, some will be retained for further examination and some will be identified as possible winners. The latter category solutions can pass directly into the next stage of your analysis-organizing solutions.

Modifications to the basic brainstorming format can provide additional stimulus. It often helps to think of a random idea which you then have to link back to the original stimulus. For example, the problem that Traidcraft is having with the wholesale side of their business might suggest 'hole' as an almost random starting point. This leads to thoughts of gaps in the distribution channels and the idea that Traidcraft might look for new wholesale channels or even develop one of its own (Traidcraft stalls?).

Reverse brainstorming forces you to think of new ideas by reversing key elements in the problem/solution situation. Could the problem conceal an opportunity? Could the solution conceal a problem? What would prevent the solution from being implemented? How might the problem clear up of its own accord?

Morphological analysis
Morphological analysis is another creativity technique which may prove useful. It requires you to look at the relationships between the dimensions of a problem. For example, Traidcraft has the problem of evaluating new product ideas. Two dimensions of this problem are newness and source of evaluation. This could give the two-way matrix shown in figure 7.2.

Examining this matrix suggests one or two possibilities. Firstly, it makes one aware that for Traidcraft there are likely to be different

	Newness		
	Old	Fairly new	Very new
Producer			
Traidcraft			
Customers			

Source of evaluation

Figure 7.2 Morphological Matrix

evaluations of new products from new producer groups and new products from existing suppliers. In the latter case the newness or unfamiliarity is rather less. Secondly, a producer group may evaluate a product highly because it is important to them that they make it. The same product may rot be highly valued by potential customers. This points to the fact that product evaluation criteria will need to be fairly complex. Thirdly, it suggests that existing products need continuous evaluation by all three groups and that perhaps new products might just be a part of the larger overall evaluation system. By forcing examination of the relationships between the important dimension of a problem, morphological analysis frequently generates fresh insights and possible solutions.

Problem redefinition
Another powerful set of techniques generate solutions by means of redefining the original problem. While this should have been done already in developing problem areas, there still remains scope for radical re-orientations of our view of a problem. Traidcraft has the problem of a restricted product range. But it is restricted only in the sense that it offers less choice than a comparable mail order catalogue or retail chain store offers to the average customer. Perhaps it should look for situations, e.g. wholesaling, limited line mail order, where the product range would not be considered restrictive.

Looking at the problem at different levels of abstraction is another way of redefining a problem. Traidcraft is short of products to sell. At a higher level of abstraction they 'need to facilitate the process by which First World countries hand over resources to Third World countries in payment for work done'. This immediately opens up a number of possibilities. Traidcraft might act as a broker for services including made-to-specification goods, repair work, sub-contracting, life experience holidays or environmental test beds.

In a similar way investment rather than consumption offers another opportunity. Individuals or organizations might be prepared to buy shares in Third World developments. When the narrow concept of a physical product is broadened, other solutions become possible.

Analogies

Analogies and metaphors can be used to escape the bonds of down-to-earth thinking. Cash flow may be thought of as analogous to water flow. You cannot use water from your reservoir to irrigate the fields (pay the producer groups) unless there is water flowing in from the catchment area (customers paying Traidcraft). Irrigation schemes have to ensure that the water gets to where it will do most good. Perhaps Traidcraft can advise producer groups on using their cash efficiently. Interest is like evaporation of the reservoir water. Perhaps benevolent outside financing of stocks might be done at lower than commercial interest rates.

New perspectives

Starting from a fresh perspective can be highly stimulating. Two techniques which do this are wishful thinking and non-logical stimuli. Wishful thinking allows you to remove constraints which prevent you from solving the problem and then asking what you would do. Traidcraft is short of products in the short term. They might like to hire a jumbo jet and fly it around the world picking up orders. Obviously this is not possible, but might not some other organization be flying aircraft back empty from Third World countries? The Royal Air Force, air cargo companies, disaster relief organizations; any of these might (but only might) be prepared to help. The trick here is to move back from the ideal to the practical without losing too much on the way.

Non-logical stimuli probably represent the most desperate form of creativity stimulus. This technique requires you to attempt to work back from stimuli (e.g. words in a dictionary) to the problem. For example, the stimulus might be·'elephant' and the problem 'long term lack of product'. Elephants never forget, and if Traidcraft haven't the product now they should 'remember' their potential customers in preparation for the time when they do. Voluntary Representatives should therefore keep a list of people who were interested but didn't buy because none of the products were suitable. This example is rather far-fetched but it illustrates the basic ideas.

Boundary stretching

Problems are usually defined in terms of their boundaries. Relaxing or at least examining those boundaries may suggest problem solutions. Traidcraft are 'short of product to sell in the short term'. However, they have plenty of some products and none of others. They should be selling what they have and heading off demand for what they haven't got. Would a new limited catalogue be a good idea? Should they start to advertise the plentiful products? Should they sell promises rather than products? All of these ideas stretch the boundaries of the original problem.

This is a rather sketchy outline of some of the creativity techniques that you might find useful. It is easy to dismiss them when you find that you can easily think up half a dozen solutions to a problem without really trying. However, you may not realize how mundane and unimaginative these are until you deliberately try to produce many more solutions using some of the techniques described here.

For those who want a more profound introduction to creativity and its enhancement, I recommend Tudor Rickards' book, *Problem Solving Through Creative Analysis,* mentioned in the section *Further Reading* at the end of the book.

7.4 SOLUTION LISTING

To illustrate the ideas discussed above, a partial solution listing is given here. Some are based on experience, some on conventional business strategies and some were generated using creativity techniques. The problems which are listed below are confined to the obvious ones which can be identified in the Traidcraft case. Other more subtle problems, opportunities and threats are left to the reader to uncover.

Lack of product short term:

(a) *expedite deliveries*
(b) *'borrow' from non-commercial competitors*
(c) *offer post-Christmas delivery*
(d) *introduce new revised catalogue*
(e) *stop promotions/warn Voluntary Representatives*
(f) *reallocate products between channels*

Lack of product long term:

(a) *quit*
(b) *buy from commercial companies*
(c) *buy from non-Third World companies*
(d) *increase purchases from traditional Third World producer groups*
(e) *extend product range to items not easily sold by mail order*

Too few producer groups:

(a) *relax purchasing criteria*
(b) *create new producer groups*
(c) *help create new producer groups*

Difficult to find producer groups:

    (a)   *promote Traidcraft to Third World organizations*
    (b)   *work with other non-commercial Third World trading organizations*
    (c)   *send board members on investigative missions*
    (d)   *set up information system*

Cash flow problems:

    (a)   *tighten up on debtors*
    (b)   *ask for more credit from suppliers*
    (c)   *look for cheap 'benevolent' capital*
    (d)   *concentrate on selling fewer products*

Stocks very large:

    (a)   *investigate customer delivery expectations*
    (b)   *improve sales forecasting*
    (c)   *improve stock control system*
    (d)   *smaller, more frequent deliveries*
    (e)   *change to higher margin products*

Short supplier credit:

    (a)   *advise suppliers how to improve their cash flow*
    (b)   *include credit requirements in purchasing criteria*
    (c)   *look for 'benevolent' Third World finance of credit for suppliers*
    (d)   *ask suppliers to tighten their belts in the short run*

Poor performance in wholesale sector:

    (a)   *increase discount*
    (b)   *increase promotion (personal selling?)*
    (c)   *concentrate on major department and chain stores*
    (d)   *change product range*
    (e)   *research retailer attitudes*

Poor evaluation of 'new' products:

    (a)   *take more care over in-house evaluation*
    (b)   *concept test with potential buyers*
    (c)   *concept test with Voluntary Representatives*
    (d)   *test market in limited area*
    (e)   *launch random product selection and check back on results*

This is an incomplete list but it is probably typical of the kind of thing you will produce initially. Just by examining the list other solutions will logically and creatively suggest themselves. If, as advised, you keep the solutions rather general in nature, you should finish up with an unordered but manageable list of solutions. The next step is to begin to organize them.

7.5 ORGANIZING SOLUTIONS

7.5.1 Evaluation Cycles

The solution list you produce will usually consist of tens of items. To evaluate each solution independently and choose amongst them is possible. However, it would be a very time consuming business. More-over, the effect of any one solution is normally dependent upon what other solutions are also chosen for implementation. This makes a solution-by-solution evaluation process very inefficient.

There is an alternative. Instead of attempting to choose the best alternatives at one go, the process can be broken down into a number of cycles. These cycles can be called evaluation cycles because at each repeat you will be evaluating the differences between alternatives and as a result making choices between them. This process is illustrated in figure 7.3.

The solutions are not tackled in a random order. This would defeat the object of the exercise. The most general solutions are evaluated first, moving down towards more detailed and more specific solutions at each turn of the cycle. This means that your solution list must be ordered in terms of how general the different solutions are. You must also recognize the interdependence of solutions and include that in your order process. One way of doing this is to create solution trees.

7.5.2 Solution Trees

Solutions exist at different levels of generality. You will discover that some of your solutions are simply describing an alternative way of carrying out a higher level solution. The problem of long term shortage of product may be solved in a whole variety of different ways including increasing the proportion of producer groups from which product can be bought, as well as finding more producer groups.

This is an example of a means-ends relationship. The higher level is the end or ends which it is hoped will be achieved. The lower level is the means by which those ends may possibly be achieved. Each means in turn can become an end for the next lower level. In this way a whole tree of means-ends relationships can be built up. At the lowest level the ends may

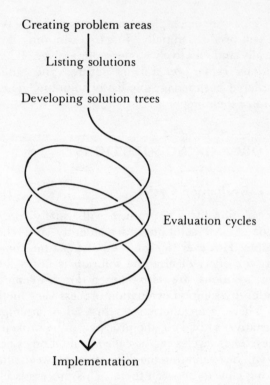

Creating problem areas

Listing solutions

Developing solution trees

Evaluation cycles

Implementation

Figure 7.3 Evaluation Cycles

be so general as to become goals and objectives, e.g., improve return on investment. At the highest level they can become as specific as you like, i.e., starting Monday, reduce credit from 60 to 30 days for customers whose annual purchases are less than £5,000.

This structure is usually called a means-end chain. However, it will be rechristened a solution tree in this book. The reason for this will become abundantly clear in the next section. A solution tree for one of the problems in the Traidcraft case is given in figure 7.4. The most general level of solution is shown at the bottom of the diagram, the most specific at the top. This example is, again, only a partial one. The dotted lines indicate alternative solutions which might have flowed from a particular higher level solution but which were omitted for convenience and clarity. The solution tree grows out of a single stem and branches out into a series of alternatives. Each point from which an alternative branch grows is called a node. As you move up the tree more and more alternatives (branches) appear and finally they become very specific and detailed (twigs).

The solution tree in the above diagram includes solutions for other problems. This is only to be expected. In developing problem areas you

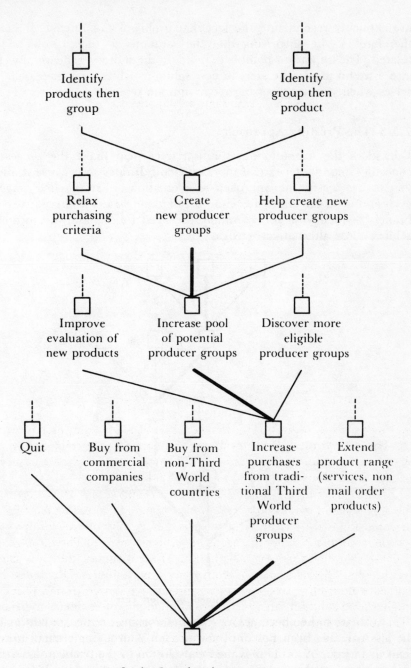

Figure 7.4 A Solution Tree

are explicitly recognizing the fact that problems are related. It should therefore not be surprising that the solutions to those problems are related. The important point is to build up the solution set carefully. It is also a useful idea to be alert to new solutions which may suggest themselves when you are 'growing' your solution tree.

7.5.3 The Pruning Approach

Why does the formation of solution trees help make the process of choosing among alternatives more efficient? It does so because it allows you to use a pruning approach to evaluation. If at the first stage of evaluation you can eliminate a number of major strategic alternatives—or branches—then you also eliminate the need to evaluate the means to achieve those alternatives—twigs.

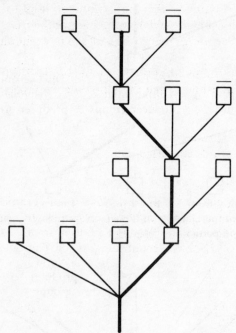

Figure 7.5 A 'Pruned' Solution Tree

Evaluation then becomes a process of working up the tree cutting out the less valuable branches until you are left with a single trunk-to-twig stem as in figure 7.5. This is the best solution to the problem assuming that you have evaluated correctly at each stage. In the example in figure 7.4 if you decide that buying from non-Third World countries is the most viable alternative then all of the other solutions, and there are many of them, can be forgotten.

In practice there are a number of ways in which a solution tree can be put together. It may, for example, be quite logical to exchange two levels in a solution tree. However, the criterion must be, 'which structure can be evaluated most efficiently?'. This means putting the most far reaching and strategic alternatives at the bottom of the tree. In this way you can hope to eliminate a lot of dead wood early in the game and so save yourself time and effort. In their early forms your solution trees will be relatively crude. They need preliminary pruning before they can be subjected to the evaluation process.

7.5.4 Simplifying

The solutions in your solution tree may be more complex than they need be. This is particularly true for solutions near the base of the tree. The more complex the solution, the more difficult it is to evaluate. This situation is rather like having twigs at the base of the tree. They make the whole process of pruning more difficult. They should therefore be removed first.

The complexity stems from the fact that solutions differ in the extent to which they are divisible. Take the following examples:

(a)   Quit
(b)   Sell fewer products
(c)   Increase wholesale discounts

Non-divisible alternatives
The first alternative cannot really be divided at all. Traidcraft either quits or it does not. There are really only two branches. In graphic terms this may be represented by a node like this:

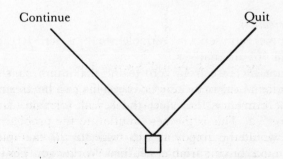

In practice there may be several alternatives of this type and it may or may not be necessary to include the *status quo* as one branch. It may have been taken care of elsewhere in the tree. Solutions like this are disparate solutions because they are different in kind, not just degree. Putting it another way, disparate solutions are like nominal or name variables.

Discrete alternatives

The second example is certainly more divisible than the first. How many fewer products should Traidcraft sell? A node for this example might look like this.

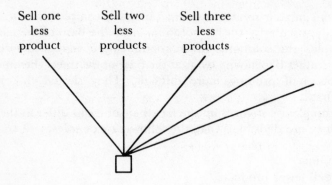

There is a different branch for each discrete deletion of one product from the product range. This might best be described as a set of discrete solutions. The overall solution can be carried out in a series of discrete alternative steps. All of them conform to the solution, yet deleting one and deleting one hundred products must rate as quite radical alternatives. Nevertheless, it is important to establish the overall liability of the general solution before looking at the range of alternatives it contains.

Variable alternatives

The final example represents a variable solution set. It can best be described as a fan of alternatives.

Any discount increase from zero to the maximum consistent with charging any price at all is included. The steps can be as small as the smallest unit of currency. In effect the set of solutions is infinitely variable.

Clearly it would be impossible to evaluate all the solution sets represented by discrete or variable solutions in one go. That is why it becomes necessary to collapse or simplify the solutions you have proposed if they are of this type and if you have suggested more than one solution

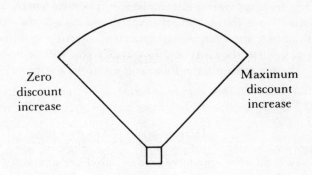

Zero discount increase

Maximum discount increase

within the same set. For example, two of the solutions at the first level in the solution tree in figure 7.2 involve Traidcraft changing its policy towards choosing producer groups. They could simply be replaced by a single solution 'Change policy with regard to choosing suppliers'. Although this is not clearly spelled out, it nevertheless represents a very different solution from the other solutions at this level. It would probably be rejected fairly quickly on the first evaluation cycle and not given further consideration unless all of the other solution branches proved to be 'dead wood'.

This raises another issue. Frequently, solutions will simply represent one alternative from a solution set. Again an example from Traidcraft illustrates this point. Suppose that one solution had been 'increase wholesale discount 10%'. In deciding on 10% you will have already prejudged the issue. You may not have allowed that solution sufficient breadth to allow it to become a good solution. Perhaps 10% extra discount would not be profitable but 15% would.

It is therefore necessary to examine the solutions you have generated to see if they can be either simplified or generalized. Don't worry about losing the fine detail of your solutions. That will come at a later stage.

7.5.5 Clarifying

Problem solving would be a very straightforward activity if one could simply try all possible solutions at once. In practice this is simply not possible. Trying one solution usually precludes trying a whole series of other solutions, though not necessarily all possible solutions. In other words, solutions are frequently mutually exclusive. It then becomes necessary to decide which among several mutually exclusive solutions represents the best alternative. The whole of the process of evaluation is devoted to this decision.

Mutually exclusive solutions

However, before deciding among alternatives, it is first necessary to make sure that they really are mutually exclusive. If you do not, two types of error can result. First, what happens if you treat alternative solutions as mutually exclusive when they are not? Essentially you will be missing an opportunity. Take for example the following group of solutions.

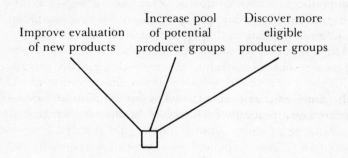

If you regarded these solutions as mutually exclusive, and in fact they weren't, then you would be missing the opportunity of employing all three solutions to increase purchases from traditional Third World producer groups.

Secondly, what happens if you treat mutually exclusive solutions as if they aren't? In this case you can almost be said to be cheating! This is a frequent error by students in case analysis. They throw everything in but the kitchen sink. While this may look impressive, it is not good practice for real life. Often students are not aware of the problem since the constraints which prevent more than one solution from being used are often subtle.

The most obvious constraints are physical and temporal. It is not possible to have a marketing director and not have a marketing director at the same time. A product cannot be called both 'Tuff' and 'Tex'. Other constraints are basically judgmental. While it is logically possible to 'research retailer attitudes' and 'increase wholesale discounts' it would seem obvious that one would not do both at the same time. In cases like these you will have to make judgements before the evaluation phase. These are necessary to clarify the structure of the alternatives to be assessed. Finally, the most difficult type of constraint is the resource constraint. It is possible to have a set of solutions which can be carried out at the same time, given infinite resources. Since this is never normally the case the limiting of resources restricts the solutions that can be implemented. This in turn renders some subset of the solutions mutually exclusive.

In one of the solution sets described for the Traidcraft case it may be possible to increase discount to retailers, increase promotion, concentrate on major department and chain stores, or change the product range. It will not usually be possible to do all four. The constraints will usually be profitability, cash flow or human resources.

Compound solutions
This problem can largely be overcome by the use of the concepts of simple and compound solutions. Simple solutions are those which involve non-divisible actions. Increasing discounts and increasing promotion are two simple solutions. Doing both is a compound solution.

Thus a set of non-mutually exclusive solutions, which are however limited by a resource constraint, can be made mutually exclusive simply by including a compound solution as another alternative. Taking an example from Traidcraft gives the following solution set. These can now be evaluated as a mutually exclusive set of alternatives.

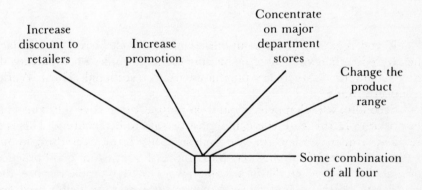

The problem of deciding which alternatives are, or at least should be treated as, mutually exclusive cannot be solved during the initial evaluation phase. As alternatives are eliminated more is understood about those that remain. This may in turn lead you to change your mind about which to treat as mutually exclusive alternatives. This is only to be expected: the process of case analysis is essentially an adaptive rather than an optimizing one.

7.6 GUIDE TO USE

Beginners may be happy to come out of step three with a list of possible solutions to evaluate. They should at least understand something about the nature of solutions and so should take in section 7.2.

The quality of your solutions will benefit from knowing what sources they derive from and these are discussed in section 7.3. Of particular help would be section 7.3.3 which describes creativity techniques.

By learning how to 'grow' solution trees as described in section 7.5, you will save yourself effort and improve the quality of your analysis. This does however require an investment in time now for returns which only become apparent later in the process.

Again you may have so simplified your approach to the case that it becomes unnecessary to cycle through the evaluation phase more than once.

CHAPTER 8

Step Four:
Predicting Outcomes

Step four requires that the outcomes of each alternative are listed and that some measure of the likelihood of each occurring is estimated.

8.1 EXAMPLE CASE—RUBACEM (UK) LTD.

In May 1978, Dr. Martin Irwin, the managing director of Rubacem (UK) Ltd., was faced with a very difficult personnel decision. John Caddy, the production controller, had, shortly after Christmas, announced his decision to take an early retirement option and leave the company on the 1st September. In the following months the post of production controller had been advertised both inside and outside the company. A very good crop of candidates had applied and a short list of 10 had been drawn up. Four of these were rejected at either the first or second interviews and two more withdrew. There remained four very good applicants from whom Dr. Irwin had to choose. However, the selection was not simply a matter of replacing Mr. Caddy. Production control had become a key problem area in the company's operation. Dr. Irwin was aware that the choice of production controller was crucial to Rubacem's future. He resolved to think long and hard about the implications of employing each of the men under consideration.

Rubacem (UK) Ltd. was a wholly owned subsidiary of Koenig Chemicals Inc. of Newark, New Jersey. It manufactured a wide range of specialist chemicals produced by batch production methods. Rubacem was one of a number of companies, largely chemical, rubber and petrochemical, that comprised the European division of Koenig which was headquartered in Brussels.

Rubacem was originally set up by an ex-employee of a major rubber company to manufacture the specialized chemicals used in the rubber industry. The small amounts of chemicals involved and the difficulty and expense of storing them dictated that batch rather than process technology was used in their manufacture. When Koenig acquired Rubacem in 1968 one of the first priorities given to the incoming managing director was to broaden the company's market base. When Dr. Irwin succeeded to the post in 1975, he continued the process until in 1978 Rubacem could fairly be described as a broadly based specialist chemical company.

This process had not been an entirely smooth one. The original sales force found it difficult to adjust to new products and markets. Most of them had been rubber industry employees. However, this problem was gradually solved as new technical salesmen were recruited and sales of new products increased. At the same time Rubacem was slowly changing from a technically expert problem-solving company to one which relied on fast delivery of fairly standard products at low prices promoted strongly by an effective sales force.

The production control department responded to the changes less well. John Caddy had been Operations Director at Rubacem before the Koenig takeover. Two years later he switched jobs with Liam O'Neill, production controller and one of the first Koenig appointees. This was done without any unpleasantness. Caddy recognized his own inability to cope with many of the changes that were taking place at Rubacem. For his part O'Neill was grateful to be able to treat Caddy as a confidante and technical adviser. He also protected the production control department from many of its critics of whom there were not a few.

In particular the internal sales office and the technical salesmen were increasingly concerned about delivery dates. Not only were they too long but they were also unreliable. The tensions between the departments were manifest. In addition, the financial director was becoming increasingly concerned about stock levels. In particular work in process continued to grow faster than sales.

Derek Mawson, deputy production controller, carried much of the day-to-day responsibility for the department and he blamed the change in product mix for these problems.

'We are making more, different kinds of products in smaller quantities than we used to. You can't expect short lead times and low stock under these conditions.' Mawson had been told by Caddy that he expected Mawson to get his job when he retired. They had both been upset when Dr. Irwin told Caddy that the post was to be widely advertised.

Dr. Irwin was not dissatisfied with Rubacem's current performance. Sales and profits were more than keeping pace with inflation and the broad spread of products meant that they were offsetting losses with gains. The recent decisions by two major chemical companies to pull out of parts of Rubacem's markets had also helped. However, he was less happy about the future. The company had to be made more efficient and production control would play a key part in that process.

Dr. Irwin was convinced that part of the answer lay in a computerized scheduling and inventory control system. He had gone so far as to commission a feasibility study from Comprod Ltd., a Manchester based computer consultancy that specialized in computer applications in production systems. Caddy and Mawson had opposed the study and vigorously attacked the consultant's report. Unfortunately it contained errors of detail which indicated that Comprod Ltd. was unfamiliar with Rubacem's technology. Dr. Irwin felt that these were minor flaws but saw no point in pushing the project forward against such opposition.

Dr. Irwin had written short notes on each of the four candidates for the position of production controller. He was reviewing those notes now, trying to envisage how each of the men involved might affect the way in which Rubacem would operate in the future.

Derek Mawson

Currently deputy production controller. Aged 38. Left school with 'A' level chemistry. Joined local chemical company in laboratories. Obtained HND at local technical college on day release. Joined Rubacem in 1965 as production planner. Made deputy production controller in 1972. Virtually runs the department now. Well liked by the plant supervisors and production planners. Knows the details of all the processes and is often asked for technical advice by production and laboratory people. A dour Northerner with no ambition beyond the production controller's job.

Michel Lepinard

Currently assistant to the divisional chief executive, Koenig Chemicals (Europe) SA. Belgian father and English mother. Educated at English public school and Cambridge (Chemical Engineering Degree—Upper 2nd). Aged 28. Fluent French and German. Joined Koenig as a management trainee and seconded to various companies throughout Europe. In 1972 joined Corporate Planning Department at European HQ. Rose to second in command. In 1977 made the divisional chief executive's assistant. Divisional chief executive would now like him to have line experience. Obviously a 'crown prince'. Strong pressure from Brussels to take him on. Looks young but very self-possessed. Has a reputation for working well with all kinds of people.

Michael Millican

Aged 45. Previously production manager of a specialist chemical division of a major competitor. The division was closed down, and Millican is currently out of work. Chemistry degree (lower 2nd) from Manchester University. Regarded as very good manager. Experience of operating, but not installing, limited computer scheduling system. Lively and articulate. Star of local amateur dramatics! Already turned down two jobs abroad.

Tom Partington

Senior consultant with Comprod Ltd. Aged 35. First in Computer Science at

Imperial College, then MSc. Joined software house then three other computer consultancies before moving to Manchester where his family live. He was the consultant in charge of the feasibility study Comprod carried out for Rubacem. Rather withdrawn and serious. References hint that he may be a workaholic. Has an exceptional track record in successfully implementing a wide variety of computer systems. Reasons for wanting job vague. Wants to 'see the benefits of what I'm dong rather than quick in and out'.

8.2 INTO THE EVALUATION CYCLE

The next stage in the process of case analysis is to choose between the alternative solutions you have developed. In the last chapter it was pointed out that it is not feasible to do this in one go. It was suggested instead that choices should be made in a series of cycles. These cycles are called evaluation cycles because on each one you will be 'putting a value on' the alternatives. This will then enable you to eliminate a number of alternatives. The evaluation cycles begin at a very general, strategic level and move up through the solution tree to the tactical and specific levels. levels.

Evaluation is best divided into two stages. The first requires that the ramifications of a solution be predicted and understood. It is not possible to fully evaluate a thing, event or course of action that is not fully understood. Few people would buy a new car on the basis of a casual glance: we would want to know much more about it even before we began comparing it with other cars on sale. In general, the more data we collect, the better we might expect our evaluation to be. This does not always hold true: sometimes it is possible to confuse ourselves by collecting *too much* data. This is a pitfall to be wary of. Nevertheless, the sheer size of the task of predicting the outcomes of particular alternative solutions will usually ensure that too little, rather than too much, data is the problem.

The second stage involves 'placing a value on' the constellation of outcomes that result from implementing a particular alternative solution. This, in many ways, is the heart of the decision process. It is usually the most difficult and complex process. It is also the one that is frequently skated over by case analysts who are afraid to 'open the can of worms'. It will be tackled head-on in the next chapter.

The process of predicting outcomes has also been broken down into two stages. The first requires that all possible, or more realistically most of the important, outcomes stemming from the carrying out of a particular solution should be predicted. Not all of these outcomes will happen. Some are almost certain: others are highly unlikely. It is obviously important to decide how likely each is to occur. It would not be sensible to give a low value to a particular solution because of a possibly disastrous but very unlikely outcome. The outcomes must in some sense be weighted in terms of their likelihood of occurring. Only in this way can a realistic picture of an alternative be obtained and used as an input to the evaluation process.

8.3 LISTING POSSIBLE OUTCOMES

Implementing a solution—for example hiring a new production controller —is rather like throwing a pebble into a pond. The ripples spread out from the point of impact. They may become less noticeable the further away they are but they are still there and may cause quite important changes to occur. Anyone familiar with systems theory will confirm that a change in one part of the system can affect almost any other part of the system. Unfortunately these changes may be unexpected and unpredictable. It will be your task to discover what they are.

The outcomes stemming from an alternative solution go far beyond the problem that generated it. The solution may help or hinder the solution of other organizational problems. It may create new problems or new opportunities. It may affect situations which are seen neither as problems nor opportunities. This realization previews a point which will be argued in greater depth in the next chapter. Solutions are primarily generated by particular problems. However, they cannot be judged solely in the light of how well they solve that particular problem. The total organizational impact of different solutions has to be compared. It may even be that a solution which is not judged best for solving a particular problem is chosen because it scores highly in terms of its effects in other areas of organizational performance. This, once again, emphasizes the need to do a complete job of predicting the stream of consequences that acting on a solution implies.

Generating outcomes from a particular course of action is, at least in part, a creative process. The creativity techniques discussed in the previous chapter apply equally well here. You will be attempting to make a series of if-then statements. Here are a number of tips which may be helpful to you in this process.

Key impact areas

Before beginning with any solution, draw up a list of key areas both within and without the organization which may be affected by, or react to, the implementation of a solution. The list might include the following:

(a) problem areas and opportunities already identified.
(b) key individuals or informal groups within the organization.
(c) functional departments and their operations within the organization.

(d) external groups or organizations including government, customers, shareholders, unions, media, competitors, etc.
(e) key operating indices such as sales growth, profitability, cost effectiveness and efficiency measures.

There will be other areas which result from your growing understanding of the organization you are studying.

As an example of using such a list, consider the solution 'employ Derek Mawson as new production controller' from the Rubacem case. This would do little to solve the current problems in Rubacem's production control department since this would simply be confirming the *status quo*. It would also probably delay, if not prevent, the adoption of a computer-based scheduling and inventory system. It would make Caddy and O'Neill happy but would probably upset the divisional chief executive in Brussels. Similarly the production, production control and technical departments would probably welcome the appointment. In contrast the sales and accounting departments would be very unhappy and view it as an opportunity lost. In general the unions and non-involved company employees would welcome promotion from within as a good general principle.

The major external impact of Mawson's appointment would probably be felt by customers in terms of longer lead times and higher prices than they might otherwise have expected. It is likely that efficiency within the plant will continue to deteriorate, stocks continue to increase and therefore costs rise faster than they might otherwise have done. Sales will grow less quickly because of higher prices and worse service than previously. Overall there may be a significant profit and profitability impact. This brief, and incomplete, example should give you some idea of how to use the check-list to generate outcomes.

Example outcome listing
As a further example a preliminary outcome listing is given below for the four alternative solutions in the Rubacem case. These are by no means the only solutions, but they are important. One or two combination solutions look reasonably attractive. For example, would any of the three external candidates work under Mawson? However, for the sake of illustration the solutions used will be those which mean employing one of the four candidates as production controller. The viewpoint taken throughout is that of Dr. Irwin.

(a) Appoint Mawson as production controller
Caddy and O'Neill happy
Divisional chief executive unhappy
Smooth takeover
Little likelihood of computer system installation

Sales department relationship continues poor
Stock position continues to deteriorate
Costs more, sales and profits less than they might have been
Need to appoint new deputy
Delivery dates unimproved
Long-term commitment

(b) Appoint Lepinard as production controller
Caddy and O'Neill unhappy
Divisional chief executive happy
Relationships with divisional HQ improve
Computer system installed but not without difficulty
Medium-term delivery date improvement
Medium-term stock position improvement
Short-term improvement of relationship with sales office
Some friction with Mawson in short-term
Mawson to quit?
Short-term friction within department and with production departments
Short-term commitment only
Costs less, sales and profits more than under Mawson

(c) Appoint Millican as production controller
Caddy and O'Neill unhappy
Divisional chief executive unhappy
Computer system installed without much difficulty
Medium-term delivery date improvement
Medium-term stock position improvement
Improved relationship with sales department
Short-term friction with Mawson
Short-term friction within department and with production departments
Medium-term commitment
Costs less, sales and profits more than under Mawson
Increased knowledge of industry and markets

(d) Appoint Tom Partington as production controller
Caddy and O'Neill unhappy
Divisional chief executive unhappy
Computer system installed with some difficulty
Medium-term delivery date improvement
Medium-term stock position improvement
No change in relationship with sales department
Continuing friction with Mawson
Continuing friction within department and with production departments
Short-term commitment
May not accept job
May resign at any time
Mawson to quit?
Costs less, sales and profits more than under Mawson

Listing outcomes in this way is rather similar to the way that solutions were listed in the last chapter, but the resemblance does not end there. Outcomes, like solutions, must also be clarified, simplified and structured. This not only helps to ensure that all important outcomes are uncovered, it is also a vital step for the second stage of the process of predicting outcomes, i.e. estimating likelihoods.

Clarifying outcomes

The first stage is to clarify outcomes. When an outcome is not certain, then it has at least one alternative. For example, one outcome listed for Mawson's appointment is 'Sales department relationship continues poor'. However, there is a small but finite chance that the relationship will improve or worsen. It may improve because Mawson would feel more secure in his job. It may get worse in line with the expected deterioration in delivery dates. These alternatives can be represented by an outcome fan as illustrated in figure 8.1.

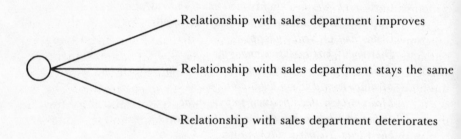

Figure 8.1 Example of an Outcome Fan

The circle is used to denote the fact that these are alternative outcomes; they are not alternative decisions. Having made the decision to employ Mawson, the outcomes are then, more or less, beyond the decision maker's power to influence. Whichever occurs will be a result of a combination of variables acting together. The best that can be done is prediction not control. That is why it is important to distinguish between the alternatives emerging from a decision node and the outcomes emerging from what is normally referred to as a chance node. Previewing chapter 9, the combination of decision and chance nodes is illustrated in figure 8.2.

This partial diagram suggests that if the decision to choose Mawson is made, then the relationship between production control and sales can go one of three ways. In this case the same outcome fan can be applied to all the other decisions too. However, the likelihoods one would attach to

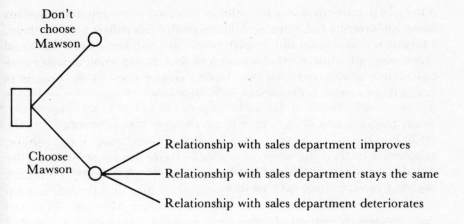

Figure 8.2 Combination of Decision and Chance Nodes

each of the events would differ very much depending on the decision as to which candidate to employ.

The outcomes in figure 8.1 are mutually exclusive alternative outcomes. To a large extent this clarifies the situation. Identifying one outcome leads to the identification of at least one other and sometimes a whole series of outcomes. This represents a major source of previously unidentified outcomes. Only those outcomes which are more or less certain do not produce outcome fans. In the case of employing Mawson, this would include the need to appoint a new deputy and the long-term commitment by Rubacem to Mawson.

Another source of additional outcomes lies in comparing the outcome lists. If an outcome appears on one list it should normally appear on the other lists since the ultimate purpose is to compare outcomes. This is not always strictly necessary. In comparing alternatives the relative differences between them is more important than the absolute. For example, the outcome 'Don't need to appoint a new deputy production controller' doesn't appear on the outcome lists for Millican, Lepinard and Partington. In a sense, not needing to appoint a new deputy production controller is the baseline from which comparisons are made. Only in the Mawson case is there a significant difference from this baseline and so it gets included in the outcome listing. The topic of baselines for comparisons will be dealt with again in the context of evaluating alternatives in Chapter 9.

Simplifying outcomes
Another important process is that of simplification. It is very difficult to handle large numbers of outcomes that differ only marginally from each

other. This problem arose, you may remember, when alternatives were being generated in chapter 7. The solution is the same in both cases. Collapse the differences into major groups. For example, in the Rubacem case the length of time the company will be committed to an individual differs from short term to long term. Clearly this could have been characterized as an outcome fan with an infinite number of increments with a lower limit of one day and an upper limit of 20 years. In practice, short, medium and long term capture the essential differences without going into too much detail. It may be that at a later stage they could be subdivided further. However, this would really only be necessary if the variable in question became a key variable which was paramount in choosing among alternative solutions.

Restructuring outcomes
The third process is that of restructuring, or more appropriately, sequencing the outcomes. This is necessary because of the ripple nature of implementing a particular solution. It is best captured by the phrase *one thing leads to another*. It recognizes that outcomes are often generated in sequence and are therefore dependent upon one another. An example is given in figure 8.3.

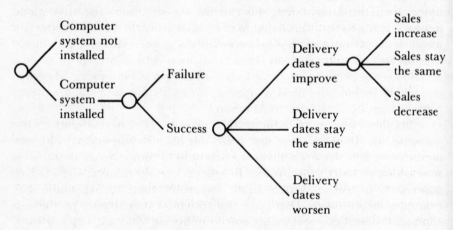

Figure 8.3 A Sequence of Outcomes

Again, only part of the sequence is shown. Successful installation of a computer system would also have effects on stocks and hence costs. Also, if delivery dates improve then the relationship between production control and the sales department is also likely to improve.

At each node all the alternatives have been given, though some may be much less likely than others to occur, e.g. it is unlikely that if delivery dates improve sales would decrease. Nevertheless it does pay to examine all the alternatives, for two reasons. First, because it helps you to understand the sequence better. For example, you might ask yourself under what conditions improvement of delivery dates would lead to sales decreasing. It could be that customers might believe that Rubacem is working below capacity and that there are good reasons for this—they might become suspicious and decide to buy elsewhere. This is unlikely but it does make you question the assumptions you are making. A second reason is that it makes the estimation of the relative likelihoods much easier and more likely to be accurate. It is important, for example, to realize that a small but finite probability of a disastrous result would often put a decision-maker off that particular solution.

This sequence illustrates the fact that many of the outcomes in the list you generate may be dependent upon just one or two pivotal outcomes. In the Rubacem case the installation of the computer system falls into that category. This sequencing also helps to generate further outcomes, for example what would happen to profits if delivery date improvement increased sales but stock increases gave rise to increased costs? Or what would happen if the computer system could not be made to work efficiently, or if its implementation took several years?

Sequencing is vital to the next stage in the process—estimating how likely each outcome is to occur. If outcomes are dependent upon each other, then their likelihood of occurring cannot be estimated independently. The probability of one occurring will affect the probability of another occurring and that relationship must be sorted out before the estimation procedure begins.

When to stop

One final point about sequencing. It is clear that you could go on for ever creating more and more detailed outcomes. In particular, if you project forward the results of taking a particular course of action, you could continue to plot the consequences far into the future. Not only does this make analysis more complex, it is not really necessary. Case studies are to some extent artificial. They are one-shot situations. In practice, problem solving is a continuous activity. It is therefore reasonable to cut short the time period over which you are attempting to predict outcomes. In real life you would take additional decisions to modify or even reverse the actions you decided were correct at the time the case describes. As the situation changes, so you adapt. It is not necessary, as is implied in the case situation, to take irrevocable decisions which will continue to haunt the organization for ever. There are some decisions which are irreversible and thus need special attention in the evaluation process. However, in most cases you should be content to make good decisions for the short term and position the organization well to face the long term. It is unfair to ask anyone to do more than that in a case situation. Even in the short term problems can occur as a result of outcomes not turning out quite as expected. You should be sensitive to such situations and develop contingency plans to meet them. This topic is covered in more depth in chapter 11.

8.4 ESTIMATING OUTCOME LIKELIHOODS

It is obvious that only one outcome from a set of mutually exclusive outcomes will in fact come to pass. Either a computer system will be installed or it will not. Unfortunately it is only after a decision has been made that we know the outcome with certainty. Hindsight is not much use before the event. Instead it is necessary to estimate how likely it is that each of the alternatives will occur.

These estimates will in almost all cases be judgemental. It is possible, in some instances, where there is a long time-series of data relating to an event which is more physical than social in nature, that the likelihood of an event can be estimated objectively. This applies, for example, to waste rates on milling machines. It may also happen that the case contains the likelihood estimates of the personalities in the case, e.g. Joe figured that there was only a 50:50 chance of a strike if the new machine was installed. However, in the majority of cases you will have to make your own judgements.

Likelihood scaling

Two methods of estimating likelihoods will be discussed here. The first is rather a rough and ready scaling method; the second involves the estimation of numerical subjective probabilities. Using the first method outcomes are classified into four likelihood groups—very likely, likely, unlikely and very unlikely. This method is illustrated in table 8.1.

It can be seen from this example that the likelihoods of estimates for a set of mutually exclusive outcomes must balance. If it is very likely that Caddy and O'Neill would be happy with Mawson's appointment then it must be the case that they are very unlikely to be unhappy. It is not logically possible to have a series of outcomes which are mutually exclusive and which are all very likely to occur. This balancing act becomes very difficult when there are more than two alternative outcomes. Is it possible to have a set of three outcomes judged very likely, unlikely, and very unlikely? Or can a 'likely' be balanced only by two 'very unlikely's? At this point the advantages of a numerical scale become obvious.

Subjective probabilities

One of the most fruitful developments in decision sciences has been the adoption of subjective probabilities judgements. For each outcome the

Very likely
Caddy and O'Neill happy
Smooth takeover
Need to appoint deputy
Long-term commitment

Likely
Divisional chief executive unhappy
Sales department relationship continues to be poor
Stock position continues to deteriorate
Costs more, sales and profits less than might be
Delivery dates remain poor
Computer system not installed

Unlikely
Computer system installed
Divisional chief executive happy
Sales department relationship improves
Stock position begins to improve
Costs less, sales and profits more than might be
Delivery dates improve

Very unlikely
Caddy and O'Neill unhappy
Not a smooth takeover
No need to appoint deputy
Short-term commitment

Rubacem Case—Alternative: Appoint Mawson

Table 8.1 Likelihood Estimates for Outcomes

subjective probability of that event occurring, given the implementation of a particular solution, is estimated on a scale ranging from zero to 1.0. A zero probability indicates your judgement that there is no possibility that the event will occur. A probability of 1.0 means that you believe that the event is certain. The scale inbetween represents any position between those two extremes. Depending on the individual, the area of 'very likely' to occur will usually be estimated at anywhere from 0.7 to 0.9. For 'very unlikely' the range might be from 0.1 to 0.3.

For any mutually exclusive set of outcomes the total of these subjective probabilities must add to 1. In other words, it is certain (probability = 1.0) that at least one of the events will occur. This makes balancing the estimated probabilities a much easier task.

In figure 8.4 (a) an outcome fan with associated probabilities is shown. This may have been the result of initially estimating the three outcomes independently. The probabilities add to more than 1.0 and therefore need rebalancing. This has been achieved in figure 8.4 (b) by reducing the probabilities of 'delivery dates improve' and 'delivery dates deteriorate'. This is not a mechanical process; it requires careful thinking and not a little judgement.

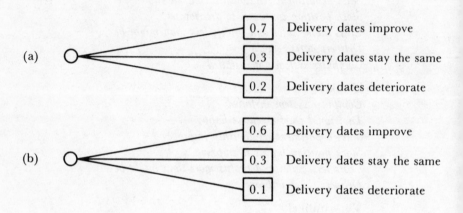

Figure 8.4 Outcome Fans with Estimated Probabilities

Estimating subjective probabilities is not an easy task. It requires practice. In particular you should attempt to think about the circumstances surrounding the situation. Consider, for example, whether or not a computer system would be installed if Mawson were appointed production controller. Dr. Irwin would certainly push for it to happen. Mawson, without Caddy's support and perhaps feeling more secure in his new role, might be less inclined to be obstructive—but why did he oppose it before? Was it fear of the unknown, or a reasonably objective assessment that the cost would be too high and the benefits too ephemeral?

It is also useful to think of the other conditions that would be likely to be operating at the same time. A new deputy production controller would be appointed. Who would he be and what effect would he have on the decision to implement a computer system? Would the sales department and the financial director apply even more pressure for improvements to take place? Would O'Neill support Mawson in the way that he had supported Caddy? Obviously there is a limit to the number of outside variables you can take into account, but remember these outcomes will not exist in a vacuum. Whichever one materializes will be determined, in part, by the conditions that surround its birth.

Multiplying probabilities

It is not only the conditions that surround an outcome but also those that are directly linked to it that are important. Consider the interdependent series of outcomes illustrated in figure 8.5: this is the sequence which was described in figure 8.3. Only one complete sequence is shown for clarity.

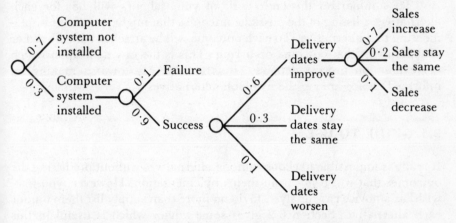

Figure 8.5 Sequence of Outcomes with Subjective Probabilities

The probabilities are those estimated for the situation in which Mawson is made production controller. It is very important to note that those probabilities are conditional probabilities. That is to say that they are the probability of an outcome happening under the condition that a number of other outcomes have already occurred or are occurring. For example, what is the probability that sales will increase given that:

    (a)   delivery improves?
    (b)   the computer system is a success?
    (c)   the computer system has been installed?
    (d)   Mawson has been appointed production controller?

It is a probability estimated under a very specific set of conditions. However, what is more important is finding a way of estimating how likely this combination of events is to occur. What we are trying to do is link the original decision to appoint Mawson with a particular and important outcome, i.e. sales improvement. This is done simply by multiplying the conditional probabilities throughout the appropriate sequence, i.e. $0.3 \times 0.9 \times 0.6 \times 0.7 = 0.11$. In other words it is estimated that, if Mawson is made production controller, there is about a 1 in 10 chance that sales will improve.

Essentially, what is being done here is to examine in a quantitative but subjective way, the conditions for a particular set of outcomes to occur. The outcomes at the end of the fan can be assigned a probability by multiplying the probabilities of the sequence of outcomes which must occur for these outcomes to have a chance of happening. In this way, the interdependence of outcomes can be captured in a quantified way and the underlying structure of outcomes fully worked through.

To summarize, the end result of your labours will be, for each alternative, a listing of the possible outcomes that might stem from implementing that alternative. To each outcome will be attached a likelihood or probability of that outcome occurring. This is the raw data upon which the evaluation process depends. It is a long way towards making an informed choice among the available alternatives.

8.5 GUIDE TO USE

It really is impossible to choose among alternatives without predicting the outcomes that will result from their implementation. However, you may wish, as a novice case analyst, to do no more than simply list them out for each alternative. Section 8.2 gives some advice which is useful in this respect.

The processes of clarifying, simplifying and structuring these outcomes obviously improves the quality of outcome statements and these are discussed later in the same section.

Outcomes have different likelihoods of occurring. Section 8.3 describes different formal ways of dealing with this problem. Clearly you must recognize this basic fact about the nature of outcomes. However, you might not wish to include a formal treatment in your analysis.

CHAPTER 9

Step Five: Choosing Among Alternatives (I)

Step five involves evaluating alternative solutions and choosing among them. The process of evaluation may vary from the simple and implicit to the complex and explicit.

9.1 EXAMPLE CASE—QUANTOCK PLASTICS LTD. (B)

On May 3rd, 1970, John Chisholm, managing director of Quantock Plastics Ltd., received a report from a Review Team he had appointed to investigate the purchase of a second hand coextrusion film casting machine. The report however did not confine itself to this issue alone. Three alternative courses of action had been identified by the team. Chisholm thought that he detected the influence of Peter Sadler here. The new corporate planner had already established a reputation within the company for stressing the broad picture and the wider issues. It was also clear that the team was divided about the right course of action. Although it was recommended that Quantock buy the machine, the recommendation was hedged around with so many qualifications that it was clearly a committee compromise. Chisholm, after a first quick reading, resolved to take the report home, and read it carefully that evening. He had two more days before he had to make a decision. This would give him time to go back to the team, individually if necessary.

Quantock Plastics Ltd. was based in the West country, near Bristol, and was the sole producer of plastic films within the Plastics Division of Finar International. Finar International was originally a manufacturer of heavy and speciality chemicals which had diversified into a number of related industries such as paper and plastics. The Plastics Division comprised seven companies involved in a variety of plastic conversion processes including blow and injection moulding, thermoforming and blowing and casting film. Finar was not involved in the production of bulk polymer so there was no question of vertical integration.

In the late 1950s Quantock had produced only blown film. This was done by melting a polymer such as polyethylene or nylon and extruding it through a thin annular ring. The result of this operation was a large, vertical, sausage shaped balloon which was deflated over a series of rollers and wound onto a reel. This tube was then slit along one edge to produce a wide (up to 120 inch), thin (approx. 1/1000 inch) film. This was a slow but cheap process both in terms of capital and labour. The main products had been heavy duty coloured polyethylene films for agricultural, building and industrial usage.

In 1962 Quantock moved into cast extrusion. In this process a curtain of melted polymer flowed from a heated barrel onto a chilled roller. The plastic cooled, set and was then wound up onto reels. Casting was more difficult than blowing and the capital costs were higher. However, the speed of production was much faster and this was the main reason for the purchase. It was also discovered that the quality of the films was higher and that the range of films that could be cast was greater.

For a year or two this potential was largely unrealized. The existing sales team failed to sell cast films into the markets for which they were suitable. This led the newly appointed managing director, John Chisholm, to appoint a new commercial director, Paul Lehrle. Lehrle's background was in packaging and he quickly developed a marketing plan for penetrating the flexible packaging convertor market. These convertors married various types of film, paper and aluminium foil to make wraps for pharmaceutical, detergent, toiletries and confectionery manufacturers. Success came fairly quickly and Quantock became one of the leading film suppliers to what was an expanding market.

In 1965 the technical manager of Quantock visited the US with a group of Plastics Division technical experts. He came back very excited about the possibilities of coextruding film. Coextrusion casting required that two molten plastic 'curtains' were discharge treated as they fell into the gap between two chill rollers. The cooled film then consisted of two bonded films. The comparative advantage of two-ply films was that the properties of the individual components could nicely complement each other. A film with good oxygen barrier properties could be married to one with high mechanical strength. A second advantage was that very thin films, which could not normally exist, of expensive polymers could be extruded onto a cheaper 'carrier' film.

Quantock quickly entered into a know-how agreement with Albany Packaging Inc. and, after a traumatic period of design, redesign, teething and commissioning problems, C1, a coextrusion casting machine came on stream late in 1966. Quantock was the first company in the UK to install such a machine, although a number of coextrusion blowing machines were operating under a highly restrictive licence from a US company. The cast films had a small price advantage over laminated (or glued) two-ply films. The growing commercial department pioneered new uses and new customers expanding beyond the packaging field into such areas as electronics (printed circuit boards) and photography (film backing). Within two years C1 was operating on three shifts.

At the end of 1969 John Chisholm appointed a C2 Review Group. They reported early in 1970 and the results were a foregone conclusion. The principal problem had seemed to be one of containing demand until the new machine could be installed. In March 1969 Finar authorized the capital and the machine with a capacity of 3500 tonnes was expected to be operational in late summer 1970. The Group also recommended that the position be reviewed midway through 1971 since market forecasts (see exhibit 9.1) indicated that it might be necessary to acquire a third machine in 1972.

On 8th April, John Kendall, head of Finar's plastics division, telephoned John Chisholm to tell him that the opportunity of buying a coextrusion machine 'off the shelf' had arisen. Finar had been contacted by Purfleet Paper who had bought a coextrusion machine but were unable to operate the machine efficiently. The sale was necessary to ease a cash flow position in the group. They wanted a decision within 10 days but would give Finar first refusal. John Kendall made it clear that he thought the machine a bargain and he wanted either Quantock or an Australian subsidiary of Finar to have it. John Chisholm was less sure and reconvened the C2 Review Group adding to in the new corporate planner, Peter Sadler, an MBA, who had recently been appointed. The composition of the group was as follows:

Peter Sadler	*Corporate planner*
Don Edwards	*Production director*
Alan Ryan	*Chief accountant*
Vernon Ould	*Market analyst*
Paul Artis	*Engineering manager*
Ted Osborne	*Coextrusion department manager*

At the first meeting they quickly agreed that 10 days was insufficient time. Don Edwards agreed to contact Purfleet and get an extension at the same time making an arrangement for Ted Osborne and Paul Artis to run a week's trial on the machine to check it out. Purfleet agreed after some discussions. The Group also agreed that the study would largely be an update of the C2 study. Vernon Ould was deputed to update his 10-year market forecasts and Alan Ryan agreed to check his value added, overhead, tax, grant and working capital estimates. This would mean some coordination between him and the technical members of the committee. Peter Sadler was to put the data together and calculate net present values for the most likely, optimistic, and least likely forecasts as required by Finar's capital application procedures. Finar used a 17% discount rate for Plastic Division capital projects. There was great pressure from John Kendall to make profitability the key operating criterion for companies in his division.

On the 27th April the Review Group met to discuss Peter Sadler's draft report. The net present values for purchasing the Purfleet machine were £445,000, £189,000 and £60,000 for the optimistic, most likely and pessimistic cases. Initially there was general agreement to recommend the purchase.

Peter Sadler disagreed. He suggested that the decision wasn't whether or not to buy the Purfleet machine but how best, i.e. most profitably, the forecast demand could be met. The Purfleet machine only had a capacity of 2,100 tonnes. A better alternative might be to build C3, based on what they had learned from C2, with a similar capacity. Ted Osborne commented that if other alternatives were being discussed then he and Paul Artis had already talked about cannibalizing the Purfleet machine. Together with C1 it could make a cheap additional machine with a capacity of about 2,900 tonnes. Vernon Ould suggested yet another alternative—triple extrusion. He had been looking at the market for this type of material and it looked promising. One or two other suggestions were made but were quickly discarded on grounds of technical or market infeasibility. After protracted discussion, Peter Sadler agreed to calculate the net present values for all four alternatives and report back to a meeting on May 2nd.

Peter Sadler made the following notes on each alternative at the meeting.

1. *Install Purfleet machine as is.* Extra capacity 2100 tonnes. Working from mid-1971. No installation problems. Extra capital (£250,000) and more labour required.
2. *Build new coextrusion machine C3.* Extra capacity 3500 tonnes. Working from mid-1972. More efficient than C2? (Improvements.) Heavy capital cost (£625,000), maybe not too much extra labour. Idle capacity for some time.
3. *Cannibalize C1 and Purfleet machines.* Extra capacity 1100 tonnes. Working from early 1972. Low capital cost (£170,000) and little extra labour. Difficult engineering problems.
4. *Triple coextrusion.* Extra capacity 2000 tonnes. (Slow speed.) Working early 1973. High capital cost (£800,000?) and extra labour. New technology, new markets.

On May 2nd Sadler reported that alternative 4 had negative net present values under even the most optimistic assumptions and it was quickly dismissed. The net present values for each of the other alternatives had been calculated by Sadler and are shown in exhibit 9.2. Alternatives 1 and 3 had, overall, better net present values than alternative 2 and the majority favoured recommending the purchase of the Purfleet machine. Sadler still had doubts. He argued that the low net present value for alternative 2 was a result of the delay in installation. This delay could result in having more accurate forecasts and therefore this alternative was less risky than the other two. In addition C3 would enable the company to develop its technological expertise. He was however overruled and agreed to write a report to John Chisholm recommending that Quantock contact Purfleet immediately.

		1967	1968	1969	1970	1971	1972	1973	1974	1975	1976	1977	1978	1979
Actual	Total market	4.8	9.2	15.0										
	Quantock sales	1.2	1.8	1.8										
Optimistic	Total market: Forecast				24.3	28.4	31.4	33.0	34.3	35.0	35.0	35.0	35.0	35.0
	Quantock: Forecast				6.0	7.1	7.9	8.3	8.6	8.8	8.8	8.8	8.8	8.8
Most likely	Total market: Forecast				21.0	24.1	26.2	27.5	28.7	29.8	30.5	31.0	32.0	32.5
	Quantock: Forecast				5.3	6.0	6.5	6.9	7.2	7.5	7.6	7.8	8.0	8.1
Pessimistic	Total market: Forecast				19.3	21.7	23.5	25.0	25.5	26.6	27.5	28.4	29.2	30.0
	Quantock: Forecast				4.8	5.4	5.9	6.3	6.4	6.7	6.9	7.1	7.3	7.5

Exhibit 9.1 Market Forecasts for Coextruded Plastic Films 1970–79 (thousand tonnes)

	Optimistic	Most likely	Pessimistic
Alternative 1	445	189	60
Alternative 2	384	131	– 33
Alternative 3	192	192	137

Exhibit 9.2 Net Present Values (£'000) for Each of Three Alternatives

9.2 EVALUATION

In chapter 7, the concept of the evaluation cycle was introduced. It was pointed out that the task of choosing among all the alternative solutions that were generated in step three was simply too difficult to achieve in one pass. It was suggested that a series of evaluation cycles be carried out eliminating alternatives at successively lower levels at each stage until just one stem of the 'solution tree' remains. Each evaluation cycle was broken into two parts. The first—predicting outcomes—was discussed in chapter 8. The second—choosing among alternatives—will be dealt with now.

Choosing among alternatives is, in principle, a straightforward process. Each alternative is first evaluated—that is to say a value is assigned to it. This value may be quantitative (profit in pounds) or qualitative (achievement of personal satisfaction). However each alternative, if implemented, would create a stream of outcomes. The values of all of these outcomes must somehow be totalled to get a value for each alternative. This problem is illustrated in figure 9.1.

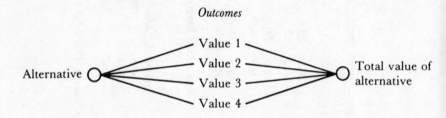

Figure 9.1 Evaluation of an Alternative

This implies a two-stage evaluation process. Firstly, assigning values to outcomes. Secondly, totalling these values to provide an overall index of value for each alternative. When each alternative has been evaluated, the choice falls upon the alternative with the highest value.

Suspending judgement
Two important points need to be made about this simple view of evaluation. The first has to do with the number of winners. It may occur that one alternative is far, far ahead of any of the others. The next evaluation cycle would then simply concentrate on evaluating which is the best way to implement, at a more tactical level, the preferred alternative. However, it will not usually be so straightforward. There will usually be two or even more alternatives which are quite difficult to choose among. In this case, it may be a better strategy to put off a decision until the end of the

next evaluation cycle. If the alternatives really are close, then the differences between them at a more detailed level can be used to decide between them. This procedure is equivalent to suspending judgement temporarily; but it isn't cost free. It means extra work in the next evaluation cycle. It is up to you to weigh the certain costs of that extra effort against the possible benefits of a better decision.

Suboptimization

The second point concerns the relationship between the original problems and evaluation. It has already been pointed out that a solution will, in most cases, have repercussions far beyond the problem it is intended to solve. It may help solve or exacerbate other problems, or it may create opportunities. So while it is true that the problem was the 'creator' of the solutions, it cannot be allowed to be the only judge for choosing between them. The solutions have to be judged in terms of how far they move an organization towards the achievement of its goals. This implies a much more general framework for evaluation than simply asking the question, 'How well does a solution solve the problem it was designed to solve?'. This last approach may lead to a difficulty which is common in problem solving, i.e. suboptimization. This occurs when problem solving is confined to one part of a system and attempts are made to find solutions only within the boundaries arbitrarily drawn by the analyst. Classical examples of suboptimization occurred in early attempts to optimize inventory levels and physical distribution systems. Analysts attempted to minimize the costs of holding stock or the overall cost of transporting goods. They ignored the interactions of both these systems with the production and marketing processes. Costs may have fallen in the sub-systems studied, but this often meant passing on problems to other subsystems with a resulting decrease in overall profits for the whole system. Operational researchers have learned from their early mistakes. The same mistake should not be repeated here.

Judgement

The process of choosing among alternatives has been described in very simple terms. In practice of course, it is much more complicated. As the chapter proceeds, refinements to the basic process will be introduced. As stated previously, you alone decide how far to go along this road, but first you should be aware of what you may be losing by stopping too early. The simpler methods of choosing rely extensively on implicit, internal judgements. You may be performing rather complex mental operations to come to your choice. It is these rather complicated processes that are brought out into the open and discussed explicitly in the later sections of this chapter. By using the techniques described there, you should accomplish two goals. The first is to be able to defend your conclusions, logically and in detail, rather than with the lame excuse, 'In my judgement, it seemed the best thing to do'. The second is to enable you to improve your judgemental skills and be able to demonstrate to your case instructor that you have done so.

What, then, are the complexities that make it difficult to decide which alternative is best? The first derives from the basic nature of values and the sources from which they can come. You will usually have some choice in this matter and this will be discussed in section 9.3. Values can be positive or negative. In other words, any particular outcome may be for or against the organization's interests. In section 9.4 a simple 'pros and cons' list is described as a way of comparing alternatives and choosing among them. The fact that different outcomes have different probabilities of occurring has already been extensively discussed in chapter 8. In section 9.5, the 'pros and cons' technique is modified to take this very important factor into account. In section 9.6 for the first time, the differing values of different outcomes will be explicitly recognized and examined. This will be done by the use of importance ratings, i.e. how important is this outcome, good or bad, to the organization?

Importance is clearly a rather vague concept. In section 9.7, explicit single criteria such as survival, cost-effectiveness and profitability are introduced to be used to choose among alternatives. But it is rare that an organization, or the individuals who control it, have a single criterion of success. In section 10.1, the problem of judging among alternatives when there are several criteria, e.g. growth, survival, and social responsibility, is examined. Finally in section 10.2 a number of methods of choosing among alternatives when the choice involves several criteria are described. Again it should be emphasized that though these techniques may seem complex they are doing no more than you do when you make a complex judgement. However, doing it out in the open means that you are less likely to make errors or cut corners.

9.3 SOURCES OF VALUES

Evaluation is the process of putting a value on something. But where does that value come from? There are three possible sources and you will have to make a choice between them.

The first source is the textbook. In any social discipline there are any number of writers who have stated what the objectives of individuals, groups, or organizations should be. For a business organization, the objectives might be profit and sales growth together with a minimum level of employee satisfaction. For an educational system, it might be the achievement of certain levels of educational achievement, measured both quantitatively and qualitatively, within predetermined cost criteria. For an architectural project, it might be simultaneously meeting environmental, aesthetic and client criteria for a given budget. In other words, the theoretical goals and objectives that organizations might, in general, pursue. This approach may be a useful one when the educational objective is for students to understand what goals and objectives an organization could have. It may also be necessary where there is so little information about the organization and the people directing it that it is difficult to predict what goals they may be seeking.

The second source is you; your values, aspirations and dreams. In this case, you simply assume that you have the power to do whatever you want to do. Deciding between alternatives then becomes a matter of what directions you would like to see the organization take. This is essentially a method for exploring your own values in decision situations: it is a relatively limited exercise which should only be carried out occasionally, as it is simply not realistic enough. Nevertheless, it is sometimes a good idea to make some very limiting assumptions—for example that everything you decide on will be done—in order to concentrate on just one aspect of case analysis. In this situation, the goal would be for you to confront your own values: the initiative is with you. You will find the comparison of your values with those of your fellow students an illuminating experience. But one word of warning: don't go off and do this without clearing it with your case instructor first. You don't want unnecessary misunderstandings to occur.

The third source is the organization itself as described in the case study. What goals and objectives does it seem to be pursuing? How would it react to this or that change in direction? In practical terms of course it is not very realistic to talk in terms of the goals and objectives of an organization. Organizations don't really have goals and objectives. However, the individuals who comprise organizations do. Thus an organization's goals and objectives can be seen as the sum total of the goals and objectives of the individuals it comprises. Summing may not be a very accurate picture of how an individual's views affect the total corporate view—some individuals are more powerful than others. This power may stem from their position in the organization or from their acknowledged experience or expertise. The weight given to a particular view will depend on the situation. An engineer, for example, would have little credibility contributing to a debate on changing the basis of accounting for inventory. Power may also stem from strength of numbers. A department will frequently have a departmental view of a situation because the people working within it are working in the same environment and see problems in the same way. Power blocks or cliques may cross departmental lines. There is in most organizations a split between loosely structured groups which might be called the 'progressives' and the 'conservatives'.

Understanding corporate values

All of these points are meant to illustrate the difficulty of judging what goals and objectives the organization is actually pursuing. It is important to put effort into understanding the complex value system of the organization you are studying for two reasons. Firstly, because it will determine the value of a particular alternative based upon how well it helps the organization achieve what you think it wants to achieve. This may not be the same value you would place on it. For example, you might recommend the continuation of a legal but deceptive advertising campaign although it conflicts with your view of the moral standards businessmen should employ. Nevertheless if, from your reading of the case, you believe that the employees of the organization would see nothing wrong with this conduct then you should recommend it to continue. Effectively, you are acting here merely in the role of an interpreter of corporate values.

The second reason for understanding the nature of corporate values is in terms of acceptance of recommendations. It will be difficult, if not impossible, to sell the organization a course of action which runs counter to its basic philosophy. It would be a waste of time trying. If, however, you incorporate the organization's values in the criteria you use to judge alternatives, then the match will be much closer and the implementation of your recommendations that much easier. This point will be covered again in more detail in chapter 11.

Key individuals' values

In order to map out the values of the organization you will need to make use of many of the analyses you have already carried out. In addition, you might wish to draw up pen portraits of key individuals, groups, or departments and attempt to assess what they are likely to be striving for. The following examples are from Quantock Plastics.

John Chisholm—seems a clear-sighted and rational decision maker; capable of decisive action; longer time perspective than many managers; good but not subservient subordinate; probably a reasonably good judge of people; delegates well; a good manager.

Peter Sadler—young and out to make a name for himself; at home with analysis and numbers; not afraid to put his own views forward; broad view of the company and its future; possibly stubborn and even opinionated.

Another point, discussed in chapter 5, must be reintroduced here. The role you decide to adopt, decision-maker or consultant, will strongly

Analyst's role

	Consultant	Decision-maker
Textbook		
Analyst		
Organization		

Source of values

Table 9.1 Source of Values and the Analyst's Role

interact with the source of values you choose to use. This interaction can best be explained by reference to table 9.1.

The consultant trying to impose his own or textbook objectives on an organization may be clear about what he wants but will find implementation difficult. On the other hand a decision-making role will make the acceptance of implied organizational goals easy, though for the analyst it will not always be clear what those are. Thus from the top left to the bottom right in table 9.1 clarity of objectives decreases as acceptance increases.

Organizational values

In any case it is clear that you must have a good idea of what the organization's objectives might be. In some cases this will be necessary because you will have to modify or circumvent them. In others because you wish to work within them. Again it is important to remember that organizational goals and objectives are summations of the goals and aspirations of individuals. However, for an organization to continue to operate, a certain core of missions and directions must be held in common. You should try, from your reading of the case, to establish what these might be. They will affect either the value you place on alternatives or the likelihood that the organization will accept it.

Such a summary has been made for Quantock Plastics and it is given below.

Quantock Plastics is an ambitious company looking for expansion in profits and sales. It is not, however, a company given to gambling. It will take calculated medium range but not high risk opportunities. It sees itself as being capable of fairly swift movement into new but related technological or marketing fields. The people are a mixture but younger, more expert specialists will come to predominate with all that means in terms of decision-making and risk-taking. There is no reason to believe that the Finar Group are likely to restrain the ambitions of Quantock. Employees might expect to make a name in this company before moving on elsewhere in the group. Job satisfaction probably comes through achievements rather than salary or status.

9.4 PROS AND CONS LISTING

The first, and apparently most straightforward, task in putting a value on an outcome is to decide whether it is, in general, good or bad for the organization. This means taking the list of outcomes you have already generated and deciding whether each one, on balance, helps or hinders the organization in the achievement of its organizational goals. The process is easily described and the output is very simple. However, the actual task is obviously not so straightforward. It relies on the analyst judging the outcome in the light of all the factors affecting the organization and its performance. Since this activity is internal it is not easy to examine. Bringing this activity into the light of day will be something that the next few sections will seek to achieve.

A tentative pros and cons listing is given below for one of the alternatives facing Quantock Plastics.

Pros	Cons
High positive internal rate of return for most optimistic forecast.	It may upset divisional chief executive.
More technological skills developed than other alternatives.	Negative rate of return for pessimistic forecast.
More efficient working with possible cost savings.	Idle capacity for some years before market catches up.
Highest capacity alternative, highest potential sales.	Late installation may mean market share lost never to be regained.
High book profit figures.	High initial capital investment.
Later installation means better forecasts.	Heavy use of design and engineering personnel during C2 installation.
Few design or installation problems.	It may upset everyone in the Review Group except Sadler.
	Lowest return on investment.

Table 9.2 Pros and Cons Listing for the Alternative 'Build a New Coextrusion Machine C3'

Balanced outcomes

Most outcomes are not too difficult to allocate. They are obviously either pro or con. There are, however, exceptions. The machine C3 has the largest capacity of any of the machines being considered. This represents both a threat and an opportunity. If the forecasts were too low then C3 would have the capacity available to make good profit and cash flow in the early years of use. If the forecasts were too high, the machine would be operating inefficiently at very low volumes. Thus this outcome of high capacity available can (and has been in table 9.2) be considered both a pro and a con. In cases like this it is best to split out the 'good' and 'bad' components of a particular outcome.

Neutral outcomes

An outcome of the type described above might be described as a balanced outcome: the 'plus' aspects tend to balance the 'minus' aspects. However, you may find that some of the outcomes you generate are not of this type but are still difficult to assign under pro or con headings. These may be called neutral outcomes. They neither support nor hinder the organization in the pursuit of its goals. It may be that this results from an inability to predict what that outcome will lead to in the future. For example, it may be that a new machine would give management an opportunity to reduce manning levels and the unions the chance to negotiate productivity increases. It is impossible, given the information in the case, to decide which would occur. Alternatively some outcomes may be truly neutral. When the decision at Quantock has been made the Review Group will be disbanded. This is essentially a neutral outcome: neither good nor bad. Taking the argument a stage further, if an outcome is neutral it cannot be used to help you decide amongst alternatives. Perhaps then a better definition of this kind of outcome is irrelevant rather than neutral. They are best ignored since they simply complicate the issue.

The process of assigning outcomes to pros and cons columns provides a useful check on the completeness of your original outcomes listing. Balanced outcomes may need to be divided. An outcome mentioned for one alternative may not have been mentioned for another alternative although it equally well applies. Outcomes may have to be combined or deleted if they are judged to have minimal impact on the organization and its progress.

T accounts

If you wish to go no further than this in your evaluation then the time has now come to choose among the alternatives. Two simple methods of doing this are suggested here, although there are obviously others. The first method is to balance your 'T' accounts. This can be done by comparing the pros and cons for an alternative and coming up with a 'net' valuation. This might be on an ordinal (very poor to very good) or a continuous (0 to 10) scale. The alternative with the best rating or score is chosen.

Key differences

Another way of carrying out the comparison is to attempt to concentrate on the key differences between alternatives. The less important and common outcomes are eliminated. The alternatives are then polarized in terms of their attributes. For example:

Alternative one.

Cheap and quick but commits Quantock to an early decision. Less capacity than might ultimately be required and no technological improvement. Best return on investment.

Alternative two.

Expensive and late but leaves time to change mind. Provides large capacity purpose-built machine incorporating latest technology. Worst return on investment but still good. Best return under most optimistic conditions.

In this way, the essential differences are highlighted and a decision can be more readily made since fewer dimensions need to be considered at the same time.

9.5 MODIFIED BY LIKELIHOOD DIFFERENCES . . .

It has already been pointed out at some length that outcomes differ in terms of their likelihood of occurrence. This should be regarded as an important way of classifying or modifying the outcomes that are being used to judge the worth of an alternative. Clearly if an alternative has a number of important and useful outcomes, but which also have a low probability of occurring, then they should be discounted by a factor reflecting this. This modification can be carried out qualitatively or quantitatively.

Qualitative likelihoods

The qualitative method would simply class outcomes as being of high or low likelihood. This classification can then be incorporated into a pros and cons listing as in table 9.3 for the Quantock alternative, 'Build a new coextrusion machine C3'. The likelihood levels in this table will normally come from the previous stage of analysis; predicting outcomes (e.g. figure 8.4). Remember that these likelihoods are not independent. The likelihoods of minor outcomes are likely to depend upon the occurrence of major outcomes. The likelihood structure resulting from the implementation of an alternative can get rather complex. That is why it is prudent to get it sorted out before the evaluation process begins. It is all too easy to allow the value of an outcome to influence your likelihood of its occurrence. In this way, analysts mould the evaluation process towards the alternative they have intuitively preferred from the beginning!

	Pros	*Cons*
Likely	More technological skills developed than other alternatives.	Idle capacity for years until market catches up.
		High initial capital investment.
	Highest capacity alternative, highest potential sales.	Heavy use of design and engineering personnel during C2 installation.
	High book profit figures.	
Less likely	High positive internal rate of return for optimistic forecast.	Lowest return on investment.
		It may upset divisional chief executive.
	More efficient working with possible cost savings.	Negative rate of return for pessimistic forecast.
	Later installation means better forecasts.	Late installation may mean market share lost never to be regained.
	Few design or installation problems.	It may upset everyone in the Review Group except Sadler.

Table 9.3 Pros and Cons Listing with Likelihood Classification

This method focuses attention on the highly likely alternatives. It makes the evaluation much more straightforward because it reduces the number of dimensions that the analyst has to use in his judgement. A more detailed approach involves the assignment of probability values as described in section 8.3 and illustrated in figure 8.4.

9.6 . . . AND MODIFIED BY IMPORTANCE RATINGS

Outcomes differ not only in terms of their likelihood but also in terms of how much they are likely to affect, for good or bad, the achievement of organizational goals. Again it must be stressed that the importance you assign to an outcome must reflect the particular values you have decided to use to judge between alternatives. The way in which you judge the importance of an outcome will be internal and judgemental. Nevertheless, it is another step along the road towards making more explicit the processes by which you favour one alternative over another.

Importance and likelihood
Importance can be treated in a similar way to likelihood. The simplest classification would use important and unimportant as the labels. Since

likelihood levels have already been estimated both factors can now be used to modify the basic pros and cons listing. This gives a two-way classification as shown in table 9.4.

Likelihood

		High	Low
Importance	High	A	B
	Low	C	D

Table 9.4 Two-way Classification of Importance and Likelihood

This classification can now be applied to the pros and cons listing for 'Build a new coextrusion machine C3'.

	Pros	*Cons*
A	Highest capacity alternative, highest potential sales. Highest book profit figures.	Lowest return on investment. High initial capital investment.
B	Later installation means better forecasts. High positive rate of return for optimistic forecast.	Negative rate of return for pessimistic forecast. Late installation may mean market share lost never to be regained.
C	More technological skills developed than other alternatives.	Idle capacity for years until market catches up. Heavy use of design and engineering personnel during C2 installation.
D	More efficient working with possible cost savings. Few design or installation problems.	It may upset divisional chief executive. It may upset everyone in the Review Group except Sadler.

Table 9.5 Pros and Cons Listing Using Importance & Likelihood Ratings

This gives quite a clear picture of where the attention should be directed. Category A outcomes, pro and con, are highly likely and highly important ones. They will therefore be the major grounds for evaluating this alternative, balancing pros against cons. This alternative has the lowest return on investment and the highest initial capital cost. It does, however, have the highest capacity alternative as well as the best 'book' profit figures (nice to report to shareholders). The key factor is that

Sadler's view that the extra time until installation will give more accurate forecasts is estimated to be not very likely. An extra year is not thought to be long enough for accuracy to improve greatly.

Importance rating
Importance can be estimated on a somewhat finer scale than important/ unimportant. A continuous importance rating can be used. This might, for example, span a scale from 0 to 1 like probability. Combining the two measures could be achieved simply by multiplying likelihood and importance ratings together. This has been done in table 9.6 where higher numbers indicate the more important and more probable outcomes. A certain (probability = 1.0) and very important outcome (importance = 1.0) would rate 1.0 on the importance/likelihood index.

Importance/ Likelihood Index	Pros	Importance/ Likelihood Index	Cons
0.54	High book profit figures.	0.54	Lowest return on investment.
		0.54	High initial capital investment.
0.50	Highest capacity alternative, highest potential sales.		
0.32	Later installation means better forecasts.		
0.28	More technological skills developed.		
0.18	High positive rate of return for optimistic forecast.	0.18	Negative rate of return for pessimistic forecast.
		0.18	Late installation may mean market share lost forever.
0.16	More efficient working with possible cost savings.		
0.12	Few design/installation problems.	0.12	Heavy use of designers during C2 installation.
		0.12	It may upset Review Group except Sadler.
		0.08	Idle capacity for some years until market catches up.
		0.08	It may upset divisional chief executive.

Table 9.6 Expanded Version of Table 9.5

There is a gap between the group of outcomes above and below 0.28. This suggests that quite a reasonable decision could be made by concentrating on balancing the pros and cons of the 'top' six outcomes.

It is important to be clear about what is and what is not being achieved by these methods. They are simply ways of highlighting the key differences between different alternatives. This helps by allowing you to concentrate your efforts. However, you still have to weigh the pros and cons of each alternative against all the others. Your decision concerning which alternative is best still rests on an internal judgement process.

9.7 A SINGLE CHOICE CRITERION

In the previous section the idea of the importance of an outcome was introduced without really discussing how it might be judged. Importance in this context was simply used as a flag. It allowed you to pick out, and concentrate your attention on those outcomes which you believed would have most impact on the organization. The next stage is to move beyond saying, 'this is important' to say, 'this is why it's important'.

An outcome, and therefore an alternative, has to be judged in terms of how much it helps or hinders an organization in achieving its goals. In the first instance this will be narrowed further to just one overriding organizational goal. The consideration of multiple goals complicates the issue. Multiple goals will be discussed in section 10.1 when some of the problems of coping with a single goal have already been dealt with.

If a single overriding organizational goal can be decided upon, then this automatically becomes the criterion for choosing among the alternative solutions you have proposed. The process then splits into two parts— choosing the criterion and measuring each alternative's performance against that criterion. But first of all, what is a criterion?

Choice criterion
A criterion is simply a measurement by which a decision or choice is made. In an examination it may be the number of marks obtained. For a manager, it might be the amount of profit his division makes in a year. For a government department it may be the level of spending. In simple situations with a single, well defined and easily measured criterion, the choice process is straightforward. Simply choose the alternative which scores the most, or least, on the single criterion—the student with the most marks, the manager with the greatest profit, the government department that spends least. For a case study, it might be the contribution of an alternative solution towards the achievement of one measure of organizational success, e.g. sales growth, profitability, cost effectiveness, employee morale or organizational survival. Before looking at how this

can be done in practice, there are some problems of measurement to discuss.

Measurement problems

Whenever a measurement is involved there are usually three forms that it can take. The first form is possession or nonpossession of an attribute. People are either men or women, an organization either gets a major contract or it doesn't, implementation of a particular solution either leads to an organization's survival or its extinction. These are on-off variables —there is no half-way house. Criteria in the form of attributes are quite useful because they are so clear cut. This point will be made again when 'hurdles and ditches' are discussed in the next section.

The second form of measurement refers to situations where it is known that different things have different amounts of an attribute but it is not known precisely how different. For example, 'very good employee morale' clearly has more of the variable 'good employee morale' than 'fairly good employee morale', but it is difficult to say how much more. Could it be 50% more, 100% more, or even infinitely more? In this case the problem lies in not having an exact measuring instrument for employee morale. Simply because it is difficult to measure something does not mean that it should be discarded as a criterion. Many, if not most, of the outcomes of the alternative solutions that you generate in your case analyses will be of this type. Can you afford to ignore the differences between a 'low' profit and a 'high' profit simply because you feel you cannot exactly quantify the difference? You will have to accept the fact that in complex situations where the future is being predicted, you will have to work with imprecise and woolly data. This is, however, one of the most important skills a problem solver can acquire.

The third form of measurement is where the scale used is continuous, or else may be considered to be continuous. Examples include sales, profits and costs measured in pounds, number of employees or percentage of warranty claims on a new product. This is the most powerful type of measurement to work with. The numbers that result from measuring in this way can be added, subtracted, divided, multiplied or operated on by a variety of mathematical techniques. If all criteria could be measured as continuous variables, many of the problems of choosing among alternatives would disappear. In the next section it will be shown that often the only way to explicitly choose among alternatives is to convert noncontinuous to continuous variables using judgement as the basis for the conversion.

Choosing a criterion

The choice of a single criterion for judging among alternatives is not usually an easy task. Consider again the sources from which it might

come (see section 9.3)—textbooks, you, or the organization you are studying. For a commercial organization, the criterion might be chosen from
among this set: survival, long term return on investment, profit growth,
sales growth, cost reduction, personal income or wealth, job satisfaction
or career growth. This is not a judgement that should be made lightly or
implicitly. Take your time deciding what criterion you should use and
state what it is in your class discussion or reports. You can then always
defend your choice of alternatives by referring back to the criterion.

Returning to the Quantock case, a defensible single criterion here
might be return on investment. Sadler has calculated the marginal rate of
return (or at least a close substitute for it) for each of the alternatives
proposed. It is a classic textbook capital investment method of appraisal.
It also seems to be accepted by Quantock's management as a key criterion
for evaluation. The fourth alternative, triple coextrusion, was
immediately dropped because of its poor marginal rate of return. The
Review Group's decision to buy the Purfleet machine was also largely
based on the fact that the rate of return was better for the two options
which involved purchase than that for the option which did not. Even
Sadler's objections were to do with the accuracy of forecasting the rate of
return rather than any objection to its use as the key criterion for
evaluation.

However, this case is rather unusual in that specific forecasts are
given for each alternative against the key criterion (see exhibit 9.2 on page
119). Taking simply the most likely forecast, alternatives 1 and 3 are
about equal, and alternative 2 is some way behind.

Qualitative criteria

If the criterion is, however, broadened to 'long-term survival of the
company' this allows a demonstration of what to do with a less easily
measurable criterion. The first step is to assess how each outcome for each
alternative is likely to contribute towards the achievement of the criterion.
This must, of course, take into consideration how likely that outcome is to
occur. An outcome can hardly contribute much to long-term survival if it
is itself rather unlikely to occur. This means starting from table 9.5 or
something similar.

Examine each of the outcomes and ask yourself, 'how is this likely to
help or hinder long-term survival?'. In particular, think through the
implications of each outcome. Look for the links between the outcome and
long-term survival. Try to estimate the impact of this outcome acting in
concert with the other outcomes that implementation of a particular
solution would create. For example, credit worthiness is an important
determinant of long-term survival. Alternative 2 implies good book profit
figures, efficient working and modern purpose-built machinery. This is
likely to impress bankers, external or internal, and mean that Quantock

could stave off cashflow problems by borrowing if a temporary problem emerged. Flexibility is another key factor in survival. Alternative 2 involves improved technical skills, spare capacity (perhaps to experiment with new materials) and a delayed decision date, all of which make this the most flexible of the three alternatives.

The power of using a single criterion now becomes evident. It becomes clear what to look for. Some outcomes can be seen to be important; others are immediately judged to be irrelevant. Upsetting the Divisional Chief Executive may involve short-term discomfort but it is difficult to see how this could affect the long-term survival of the organization.

Choosing an alternative

In many cases, using the razor's edge of a single criterion the choice will be fairly evident. Some alternatives will disqualify themselves because they score low on the criterion. In other cases the differences between alternatives will be so large as to make the choice inevitable. When differences are small, it may be necessary to carefully rank the alternatives on your judgement of their expected performance against the criterion. In extreme cases you might decide to scale alternatives using numerical values. In essence, what you would be doing would be to ask yourself the question 'How would I rate, on a scale from 1 to 10, the contribution that this alternative would make towards improvement in the chances of long-term survival?'. This procedure would help you to concentrate your attention on what you believe are the most important differences between alternatives in terms of their effects on the single criterion of success.

CHAPTER 10

Step Five: Choosing Among Alternatives (II)

10.1 MULTIPLE CHOICE CRITERIA

If you followed section 9.7 carefully you may have begun to suspect that using a single choice criterion is not so straightforward as it looks. There are two reasons why using more than one criterion makes for better decisions. The first is that organizations and individuals rarely pursue single goals. The second is that it is often difficult to link the outcomes stemming from an alternative with their effect on a particular goal. Sometimes it is necessary to substitute several intermediate goals for one ultimate goal. Both of these reasons for moving beyond single to multiple criteria will now be examined in detail.

In practice people use multiple criteria in judging between alternative solutions without realizing it. Imagine a company with the problem of a factory making an unsuccessful product. One of the alternatives would be to burn it down and collect the insurance money. The problem would be solved: the company would no longer have a factory selling an unsuccessful product. But that solution is antisocial, immoral and illegal. In ruling out this alternative you would be implicitly using criteria beyond the simple 'solves the problem as described in the case'. As a less extreme example, consider the alternatives evaluated in section 9.7. The single criterion used was that of long-term survival. Suppose an alternative had been proposed which ensured long-term survival but which involved employing illegal immigrants. On a single criterion it would win hands down—but at what cost?

Goals and constraints
Both of these examples are meant to demonstrate that we use multiple criteria in all our decision-making. Individuals and organizations want to achieve a mixture of different goals. One goal may predominate at any one time but other goals cannot be ignored. A course of action which supports the pursuit of one goal to the exclusion of others will not, in general, be chosen. Goals may be both positive and negative. We are

usually clear about what we want more of. We are usually even clearer about what we want less of, or indeed none at all. Goals of this kind are usually called constraints. These are directions in which we do not want to go; areas in which we would not want solutions to take us.

Conflicting objectives

Another point is that very often organizations and people have conflicting objectives. Individuals wish themselves health, wealth and happiness; not just one but all three! We wish for friendship, but do not wish to have our personal liberty curtailed. We want to be rich, but not at the expense of our leisure time. We wish to help others, but there is a limit to the amount of tax we would agree to have deducted from our salaries.

This is quite complicated enough. However, the problems are made much more difficult because the decision usually concerns not just one person but many. In discussing cases, the unit of analysis has been the organization. It is true that for some small organizations this essentially means one man—the owner. However, these cases are rather rare. Even in the Quantock situation there are several people to consider. When there are a number of people who may be involved in the decision, then they will all bring their own particular values into the decision process. Very frequently these values will differ. One person may value stability, another may value growth, while a third may value excitement.

Educational objectives

Even where there is one very clear cut single criterion, it can be argued that a second should always be added to it. This second criterion is that of educational value. To include this we must take a step back from the process. Why are you doing this case study? Obviously in order to improve your analytical and creative skills. However, alternatives may differ in the extent to which they allow you to do this.

For example, two alternatives that often appear in case presentations are to appoint somebody to sort it out and to collect more information. Of course these are often legitimate and important alternatives. However, they appear rather more often than is warranted by the circumstances. They both score rather badly on the criterion of educational value. If someone is appointed to sort out the problem, this absolves the analyst from doing so. If more information is required, then it is easier to suggest how this might be done rather than making, and defending, a decision based upon the information actually available. If a case analyst wishes to get experience in solving organizational problems he may reject alternatives like this on educational grounds. In effect you will be saying 'I realize that other alternatives were probably as good but I chose to pursue this one, because developing it I thought I would get more mileage out of the case'. A case instructor will usually support a student doing this provided that it is done explicitly and with advance warning.

Uncertainty

The second reason for multiple criteria is uncertainty. This uncertainty can come from two sources. Firstly, it may be difficult to get a precise measure of a particular organizational goal. Secondly, it may not be easy to predict how much a particular alternative contributes to the achievement of a particular organizational goal. Both of these uncertainties can be resolved by splitting a single goal into multiple subgoals.

Suppose one goal of an organization is stability. How can this be measured? Employee turnover rates? Constant profit growth? Continuing to operate within existing technology? In practice it is unlikely that just one variable can capture the flavour of the goal as originally intended. Several measures will usually be needed. All of these may be insufficient in themselves, but together they equal the original goal and provide a reasonable measure of it. Figure 10.1 illustrates this idea in relation to the corporate goal of stability. These subgoals in effect are substitutes or proxies for the original goal. Not unnaturally they are therefore called proxy goals. They 'stand in' for the important goal because it cannot be measured directly.

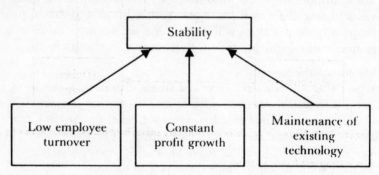

Figure 10.1 Proxy Variables for the Organizational Goal Stability

The second source of uncertainty is similar to the first. The difference is that the goal is easy to measure but the ways in which it might be achieved are not. Take for example the goals of sales growth or profitability. Both are easy to measure, what is difficult is predicting how a particular alternative course of action will affect these variables. Again, the answer is to break down the main goal into a series of subgoals as in figure 10.2 for the goal *sales growth*. Thus, you would expect sales growth if prices rise, if new customers are obtained and if existing customers buy more. The effect of any one alternative on these proxy goals is easier to measure than the effect on the ultimate goal. Of course, it is always possible that good performance on one subgoal would be more than offset by poor performance on another. For example, increasing price might, and usually will, reduce both the number of new customers and the usage of existing customers. You will need to watch for these effects when judging between alternatives. Nevertheless, the process of creating proxy variables will alert you to the different routes by which a particular course of action can affect a particular organizational goal.

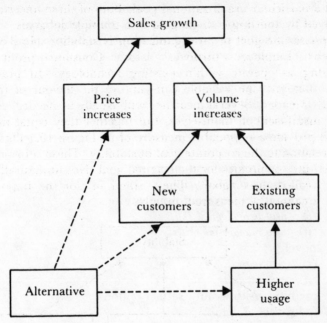

Figure 10.2 Proxy Variables for the Organizational Goal Sales Growth

Generating multiple criteria

Now that the reasons for multiple criteria are understood, a practical method for generating them is required. The place to start is with a general list of the goals of an organization taken from a textbook, from your understanding of the organization and the people in it, or from what you would want an organization to achieve if you were in charge. Refer back to section 9.3 for a detailed discussion of these three sources of organizational goals.

For Quantock the following short-list might have been generated by John Chisholm from his understanding of the company and the people within it:

(a) long-term growth
(b) efficiency
(c) increasing employment opportunities
(d) novelty

(e)   medium risk/medium return options
(f) (educational value)

This list could have been longer but it encompasses the major elements of the values ascribed to Quantock as summarized at the end of section 9.3.

The next step is to examine each of these objectives—soon to be criteria—to see whether they need to be replaced by proxies. The original Quantock list has been expanded to the one given below.

(a)   long term growth
      (i)   *increased cash flow*
      (ii)   *increased sales*
      (iii) *increased profits*
(b)   efficiency
      (i)   *increased return on investment*
      (ii)   *improved productivity*
(c)   increased employment opportunities
      (i)   *new technological skills*
      (ii)   *new managerial skills*
(d)   novelty
      (i)   *new markets*
      (ii)   *new products*
(e)   medium risk/medium return options
(f) (educational value)

It is important to remember that these objectives are not equally important, nor do they necessarily coincide. An alternative may offer increased sales, but little in the way of increased profits or cashflow. The trade-off of one goal against another in making a choice is discussed in the next section.

This will not necessarily be the final version. An initial examination may reveal overlaps or omissions. There is no mention of margins. Are they only to be considered as a link between sales and profits? Aren't 'new products' and 'new technological skills' more or less synonymous? Changes can, of course, be made at this stage. However, you will normally find that when you begin to use these objectives as criteria, their deficiencies will be revealed. You may discover that unlikely alternatives will score better than the ones you thought the most suitable. This will usually be because you have omitted a key criterion which only occurs to you when a decision has to be made. Alternatively you may find that some criteria have no discriminating power at all and can be omitted. The choice process should be seen as adaptive. It should not degenerate into simply a mechanical procedure.

10.2 METHODS OF CHOOSING USING MULTIPLE CRITERIA

10.2.1 The Choice Problem

The problem you have to face is essentially the following: to choose among a small number of alternatives each with a number of predicted outcomes by judging how they help in the achievement of a number of alternative goals. This can probably be illustrated best by means of a matrix, as shown in figure 10.3.

	Criteria				
	C1	*C2*	*C3*	*C4*	*C5*
A1	p11	p12	p13	p14	p15
A2	p21	p22	p23	p24	p25
A3	p31	p32	p33	p34	p35
A4	p41	p42	p43	p44	p45
A5	p51	p52	p53	p54	p55

Figure 10.3 Multiple Criteria Choice Process

The alternatives, e.g. 'build a new coextrusion machine' are A1 to A5. The criteria against which they are to be judged, e.g. 'Efficiency' are shown as C1 to C5. The performance of an alternative (A1) on any criterion (C3) is shown as p13. For example, how would building a new coextrusion machine contribute to the efficiency of Quantock?

The choice process described here is in two parts. The first part attempts to eliminate certain alternatives before any comparisons are made. In some situations, all but one alternative can be thrown out and therefore the choice has been made by a process of elimination. The second part, if it is necessary, requires a comparison to be made among the surviving alternatives by combining their performances on all the criteria and choosing the alternative with the best overall performance. The term *combining* is deliberately vague. It does not necessarily imply a simple summing process: it may be more complicated than that. However, the overall position is simple—the best combined performance on all criteria wins. The best input into these two processes would be the T accounts described in section 9.5, an example of which is given in table 9.3. This is essentially a summary of the pros and cons of each alternative modified by the likelihood of their occurring. It provides, at a glance, an excellent basis for judging the performance of an alternative on any criterion. In particular, it reminds you that all outcomes are not equally likely. The probability factor must be carried forward into the judgement of performance against criteria. A very favourable performance must, for example, be downgraded if it is unlikely to occur.

10.2.2 Hurdles and Ditches

It is common in popular sporting events to limit the entry. This is done so that the contestants have the best conditions under which to be judged. The limitation is achieved by specifying that only applicants who have previously surpassed a certain performance level may enter. A similar principle may be used in evaluating alternative solutions in a case study. Only the solutions which clear certain hurdles or ditches will be allowed to continue on to the full comparison procedure.

Hurdles and ditches can operate in one of two ways. In the first type, an alternative must exceed a certain value on the criterion. For example, using the education criterion, an alternative must allow a student practice at developing a complete action programme. An alternative described as 'sell up' would not meet this criterion and would be eliminated. The second type of hurdle or ditch eliminates certain alternatives if they do exceed a certain value on a criterion. Any high risk option, e.g. 'move into microelectronics' would automatically be eliminated from consideration in the Quantock case. It exceeds even the medium level of risk tolerance that Quantock management is believed to possess. Hurdles and ditches can be created by examining each criterion and putting a maximum and/or minimum on each. This has been done in table 10.1 for the Quantock criteria developed in the previous section.

Some criteria cannot be assigned maximum and minimum criteria. This is no problem since it simply means that you will have less chance to prune out unwanted alternatives early on. Note that the first three items in table 10.1 have both maxima and minima. This, in a sense, is a reflection of the need for stability. Too much growth could be as unacceptable as too little. Note also that some criteria have a minimum and some have a maximum. This clearly depends on how the criterion is defined.

	Minimum	*Maximum*
Increased cash flow	0% per annum	20% per annum
Increased sales	0% per annum	25% per annum
Increased profits	0% per annum	50% per annum
Increased return on investment	Positive net present value	—
Improved productivity	0% per annum	35% per annum
New technological skills	?	?
New managerial skills	?	?
New markets	—	10 per annum
New products	—	3 per annum
Medium risk		
Educational value	Must permit complete analysis to be made	

Table 10.1 Maximum and Minimum Values for Criteria

Remember that the fourth alternative, triple coextrusion, was eliminated because it failed to meet the return on investment criterion which in this case was defined in net present value terms with a 17% discount rate. Again it should be pointed out that these values should be used adaptively. Try and set out and see if they eliminate any alternatives. If they do, are you happy that they have or do you feel they need to be changed?

Worst or best

A second form of elimination is possible. This occurs when an alternative clearly performs worst on all criteria. There is no way in which it can, because of the differing importance of different criteria, compensate for bad with good. It is definitely the worst and can be dropped.

The reverse situation is less likely but more interesting. It is possible to find a situation where one alternative outperforms all others on all criteria. In this case it cannot be bettered and the choice is obvious. This rarely happens in practice simply because most alternatives have good and bad points. The weighing of pros and cons in these circumstances is dealt with in the next section.

10.2.3 Weighing Overall Performances

The alternative with the best overall performance is the one which will be recommended to the organization. How is overall performance to be judged though? As with many of these procedures the task is twofold. First, the individual performance of each alternative on each criterion must be judged, i.e. a value must be assigned to each of the ps in the matrix in figure 10.3. Second, these values must be combined in some way to give a single overall value. The alternative with the highest value is the alternative of choice.

Combining performances

These procedures are not necessarily straightforward. Consider the following example concerning two alternatives. The first is expected to boost return on investment to 15% over a five-year period, the second to 12%. The first alternative requires a short term cash payment of £500,000, the second does not. Which of these two alternatives should the organization choose? Consider first the performance of the alternatives on the two criteria return on investment and cashflow. Since neither alternative is superior on both criteria, some way must be found for combining their performances. This is made difficult by the fact that the criteria use different measures. Return on investment is a ratio and cashflow is measured in money terms. They cannot simply be added. Some way must be found of converting both these values to a common basis.

The simplest method is to use a common scale for each criterion. This will usually be a 1 to 10 scale with 1 indicating a very poor performance on this criterion and 10 a very good performance. The scores on any one criterion are best estimated by examining all the alternatives together. Then you have some measure of the range of the values involved. This in turn makes it easier to allocate particular alternatives to particular points on the scale. For the example used above, the following values may have been decided upon.

	Criteria		
Alternatives	*Return on investment*	*Cash flow requirement*	*Total*
One	8	5	13
Two	5	10	15

Table 10.2 An Example of Choosing Using Unweighted Criteria

Weighting criteria

These numbers can now be added and the second alternative comes out best. But this leads to another difficulty. The above method of combining the performances of different alternatives on different criteria assumes that all criteria are equally important. This is obviously not the case: some criteria are far more important than others. This can be reflected by weighting each criterion to reflect its importance. Thus in the example given above, if return on investment is regarded as twice as important as cash flow, then it could be given a weight of 2. Alternatively a total weight value of 100 could be allocated among the criteria. This method is shown in table 10.3.

	Criteria		
Alternatives	*Return on investment*	*Cash flow requirement*	*Total*
Weight	67	33	
One	8	5	701
Two	5	10	665

Table 10.3 An Example of Choosing Using Weighted Criteria

Alternative one now becomes the choice.

This method is not without its drawbacks. It assumes that the choice is best made by a linear additive $(ax + by)$ combination of the performance of the proposed alternatives on different criteria. It is entirely possible that non-linear functions would be a better representation of the way peoples' values cover the alternative values. It may also be that performance values should be multiplied rather than added. This method penalizes the alternative with a good overall performance marred only by one or two bad points. There are a vast variety of choice·rules that could be used. In effect, the more sophisticated rules are attempting to give a more accurate representation of how decision makers combine alternatives with different values and come to a single overall judgement.

However, in practical terms, these sophistications require more time and data than are normally available in a case analysis. The simple linear additive method works quite well to spell out the crucial tradeoffs that have to be made when coming to a final judgement. It is easy to understand and it is straightforward to experiment with the scales and weights if the results do not seem to accord with our intuitions.

Choice procedure—an example

The procedure, then, is as follows. The list of criteria obtained as described in section 10.1 must first be weighted. As an example, this has been done for the criteria generated by the Quantock case. A shortened list has been used to simplify presentation.

	Criteria	*Weights*
C1	Sales growth	25
C2	Profit growth	15
C3	Return on investment growth	35
C4	New technological skills	5
C5	Risk	10
C6	Educational value	10
		100

Table 10.4 Criteria Weights for the Quantock Case

The first weights assigned will usually require adjusting until a pattern that seems to map the values of the organization emerges.

Each alternative is now rated on a scale from 1 to 10 on each criterion. Again it should be emphasized that the T accounts described in section 9.5 are the best summary of the outcomes expected from each alternative and their likelihood of occurring. Remember that the likeli-

hood must figure prominently in the assessment of the value to be given to
an alternative in relation to any criterion. In a sense each outcome is
being weighted not only by how much it contributes to a criterion but also
how likely it is to occur.

Having weighted the criteria and scaled the alternatives on those
criteria, a matrix like that shown in table 10.5 can be constructed. The
scores for each alternative can then be calculated and the overall best
solution determined. If a number of these evaluations are to be carried
out, it is useful to draw up a blank form and copy it.

Alternatives	*Criteria* *Weights*	C1 25	C2 15	C3 35	C4 5	C5 10	C6 10	*Weighted totals*
A1 (Buy Purfleet machine)		7	7	8	2	6	8	710
A2 (Build new coextrusion machine)		9	8	6	8	6	8	735
A3(Cannibalize Purfleet and C1)		5	6	9	4	6	8	690

Table 10.5 Example of an Evaluation Matrix—Quantock Case

Perhaps it might be worthwhile commenting in detail on this evaluation matrix. On sales growth the results are in line with the capacities of
the three machines. Profit growth is highest for A2 because it is planned to
be installed later, the discounted cash flow is less than either of the other
alternatives. Hence its poor performance on C3. A2 will clearly allow
enhancement of technological skills within Quantock but the weighting of
C4 is small and this is likely to have little effect on the overall positions.
Because A2 involves a delayed decision it might be expected that this
would be the least risky proposition. However, it has already been judged
that this is not likely to significantly affect the accuracy of sales forecasts.
In addition the capacity of the machine and the capital tied up in it
represent a bigger risk than that involved in alternatives 1 and 3 in the
case that the likely level of sales do not materialize. These factors balance
out to an assessment that all three ventures are equally risky. Again there
is little to choose between the alternatives in terms of educational value.
Each will require the creation of detailed action plans to ensure that the
alternative as set out will actually come to pass.

In the end alternative 2, build a new coextrusion machine, seems to
have come out on top. Despite the fact that it is worst on return on investment, its performance on other criteria more than compensates. As
mentioned earlier, you may decide that this has occurred because the
weights or scale scores are not quite right.

You are quite at liberty to work through the exercise again—it doesn't take long to repeat—with new values. In addition, you may decide that two scores are so close that it makes no real sense to choose a single winner. In this case, as discussed earlier, it might be sensible to carry two alternatives forward to the next stage of the evaluation cycle.

10.3 GUIDE TO USE

At the very minimum, a student should decide what values he will use in choosing among alternatives (section 9.3). Failure to do so very frequently leads to inconclusive case reports and discussions. The next step, of producing T accounts, does not take much extra effort, but very quickly clarifies the differences between alternatives (section 9.4). Modifying these accounts in the light of the different probabilities that different outcomes have of occurring is a useful additional step (section 9.5). Beginning case students will not wish to go beyond section 9.6 which discusses combining importance ratings with likelihood estimates.

Sections 9.7 to 10.2 represent a practical approach to a very complicated decision process. This involves choosing among alternatives with different outcomes of different likelihoods against not one, but several different criteria. This is the crux of the process which we call judgement. Students should aim to try out all these techniques discussed in these three sections before they complete a case course. They not only provide practical techniques for decision making, but also provide individuals with personal insights into the process.

CHAPTER 11

Step Six: Rounding Out the Analysis

Step six bridges the gap between the process of analysis and communicating the results of that analysis. It involves detailing and making contingency plans.

11.1 DETAILING

In chapter 7 the parallel concepts of evaluation cycles and solution trees were introduced. It was suggested that these were necessary simply because evaluating all the alternative solutions was simply too difficult to achieve in one attempt. To remind you how these concepts work figure 7.5 is reproduced here (figure 11.1).

A solution tree is simply a way of structuring alternative solutions. The most general and strategic solutions are at the bottom or trunk. The most specific and tactical solutions are at the top (twigs). At each level there are a number of mutually exclusive solutions stemming from a node. The purpose of an evaluation cycle, as described in detail in chapters 7 to 10, is to 'prune' out all but one of these solutions. In the next cycle the pruning is carried out at the next node in the solution tree. In this way a compound solution is built up from trunk to twigs, from ends to means.

Clearly an important decision is when to stop. It would be possible to go on *ad infinitum* adding more and more levels to the solution tree and evaluating the options at each level. The question is, 'how much detail is required?'. Basically this comes back to the perennial problem of depth versus breadth. With a given amount of time at your disposal you must allocate your effort between these two competing ends.

Breadth and depth

A broad analysis would be one which extensively examines a large number of competing general solutions or strategies and chooses amongst

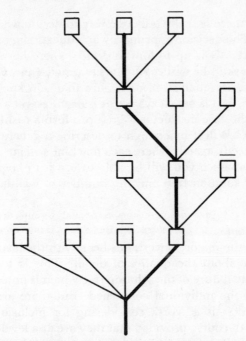

Figure 11.1 A 'Pruned' Solution Tree

them but which says little or nothing about how they might be implemented. An analysis in depth would devote less time to choosing among solutions at the general level and more to working out the details of how they might be implemented.

Beginners at case analysis frequently inhabit the extremes. It is not unusual to see statements like, 'The company should do more research', or, 'They should pay more attention to industrial relations'. This is certainly taking the broad view. But most case instructors would not resist the temptation to ask, 'what kind of research?' and, 'what kind of attention to what aspect of industrial relations?'. In other words they are asking for more detail; less breadth and more depth. To be accurate the kind of student who produces statements like those mentioned above is hardly likely to have much breadth to his analysis either but that's a problem for the case instructor.

There is a second type of student who likes to get straight to the heart of the matter. He ignores all the major strategic issues and gets down to the detail of writing copy, devising timetables or designing machine modifications. This type of student frequently has considerable industrial experience and is presumably repeating the behaviour which was normal in the work situation. A case instructor in this situation would usually attempt to pull the student back from the problem and get him to take the broad view.

In practice there is really only one way to decide what level of detail is appropriate. The decision is primarily an educational one and lies with the case instructor. It is up to him to decide where he wants to put the emphasis; which skills he wishes students to practise in which situation. It is your job as a case analyst to make sure that you know what level of detail is required. If it is not clear, ask. It is useful to get a specification by example. Does the case instructor want a pro forma cashflow forecast for the new product? Will it be enough to describe a general factory layout rather than to specify exactly where each machine will go? Having got this information in advance you will be able to use it to help determine the 'height' of your solution tree and the number of evaluation cycles you need to do.

Quality of detail

Up to this point the major concern has been with the level or quantity of detail, but what about the quality of detail? This is to a large extent determined by the nature of the solution tree which is in turn a function of the creativity of the individual concerned. But there are some general kinds of detail that it is worth considering for inclusion in your case solution. This is of course provided that they are at a level consistent with that required by the case instructor. These types of detail are in very general categories and each will be discussed in turn below.

Timing

First of all it is worth considering the timing of the actions that you will be recommending. It may be enough to simply run through the events to see if there is a feasible timetable. Having convinced yourself that there is, you may not even include it in your report. However, you may discover that your pet solution requires reworking in order that a particular sequence of events occurs in a particular order. You may have decided for example to use the annual exhibition of furniture manufacturers to launch your new easy chair only to discover it really can't be researched, developed and manufactured in time. Timing is frequently ignored by case analysts but it is of course a very important factor in determining the success or otherwise of a particular solution. Collect extra marks by including a time scale in your presentation.

Responsibilities

Organizations don't implement solutions, people do. An important point of detail is to ask yourself, 'Who will be responsible for which part of the proposed plan of action?'. This may be a fairly straightforward allocation of responsibility to existing departments and/or individuals. On the other hand you may discover that your solution implies major reorganization. If this is the case you may have to rework your evaluations since this is an outcome that you missed on the first run through. Making a department responsible for the whole, or even a part, of your solution implementation does not mean that it will be carried out. You may therefore consider how your plan might be presented to its implementors so that its chances of success are enhanced. This may mean no more than careful explanation and consultation. Alternatively it could mean a change in the entire reward system of the organization.

Resources

Although they should have been considered in the evaluation of the solutions, resources are a factor which might usefully be examined at the detailing stage. Students frequently forget that money, men and materials are limited in an organization, at least in the short term. Beginning case students are frequently embarrassed by questions such as these. How is this going to be paid for? How many extra personnel will be needed? How will managers cope with the extra work load? Is there space on the current site for the new development? Are high street sites readily available?

Feedback

While it is true that you cannot implement your solutions and get feedback on their performance, that does not mean that you should ignore feedback entirely. Part of the detailing of your solution should include provision for feedback. This may be no more than a listing of key parameters, e.g. sales, staff turnover, cash flow, profit. Alternatively, you may feel it necessary to specify a continuing research programme which will allow detailed monitoring of the implementation of your solution.

Disadvantages

In the evaluation cycles you will have become aware of the advantages of your preferred solution. When sketching in the detail you should keep these factors in mind. In particular, it is important to ameliorate the disadvantages as much as possible. For example, if a particular solution set means fewer employees then a detailed plan for redundancy negotiations and payments, redeployment, early retirement and so on should be worked out. This will never convert a disadvantage into an advantage but at least it should lessen the impact.

All of these types of detail should, in truth, have been picked up in the development of solutions. However, it is too much to expect that this will always happen. To consider them again at the detailing stage is to provide a safety net.

11.2 CONTINGENCY PLANNING

It has been a repeated theme throughout this book that the case method suffers from being a static learning experience. The case situation is a snapshot at one point in time. Case analysts have to make far-reaching, grand slam, one-off decisions which it is hoped will set the organization on the right path far into the future. In practice, decision making is rarely carried out in this fashion. It is more usually a sequential, adaptive process. Managers take a small decision, look at the effects, take another decision and so on. Rarely do they have to keep all the balls in the air at once. In addition they can usually reverse a decision before its consequences become disastrous.

It seems only fair that case analysts should be allowed some measure of latitude in their decision-making to bring them closer to a real world situation. This can be done by means of contingency planning. It is not without its costs. The whole process of case analysis becomes more complex and the learning experience may not be quite so useful in some ways. Nevertheless it is an option that should be carefully considered.

Unconditional decision-making

The method of solution evaluation described in chapters 7 to 10 required that unconditional decisions be made. The uncertainty inherent in making decisions about the future was handled by weighting possible outcomes by their subjective probability of occurring. The option of changing one's mind was not allowed. This essentially is what contingency planning is about. It may best be illustrated by a diagram such as figure 11.2.

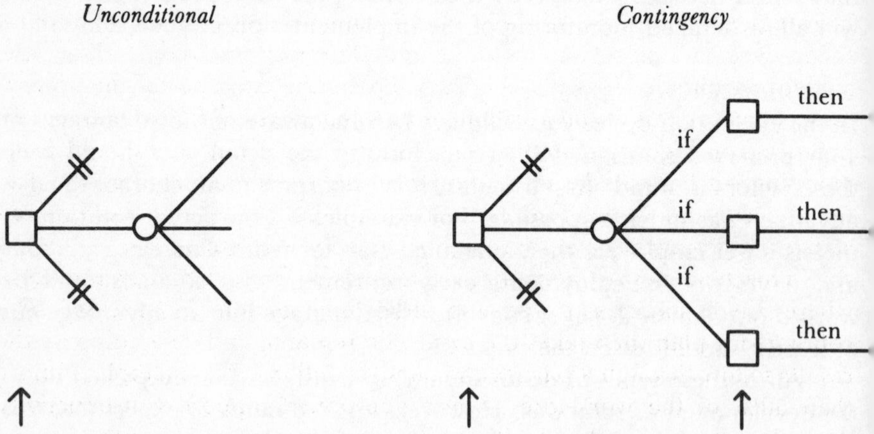

Unconditional   *Contingency*

Figure 11.2 Comparison of Unconditional and Contingency Planning

Unconditional planning requires that an unconditional decision be 'case time'. This decision takes into account the fact that each decision has a number of possible outcomes each with an estimated probability of occurring. The solution with the highest predicted value is chosen and no conditions are placed on that choice. It is final and irrevocable. The value of taking that decision will only become known when a particular outcome actually comes to pass.

Conditional decision-making

By contrast contingency planning allows for conditional decision-making. At 'case time' a decision can be made as to which general course of action to take. But when the outcome of taking that decision is known then a second unconditional decision comes into play. This means that the plan responds, albeit in a preprogrammed way, to changes in circumstances. The original conditional decision is couched in 'if . . . then' terms. If a particular outcome occurs, then the decision is to do this. If a different outcome occurs, then the decision will be to do something else.

This corresponds much more closely to the way that decisions are actually made. However it differs in one important aspect and this reveals a major weakness in the technique. With contingency planning it is necessary not only to identify the outcomes of a particular course of action in advance, but also to decide what to do in the light of that information. In real life the decision can wait until the outcome actually occurs. Thus contingency planning is much more complex than either real life decision making or unconditional planning.

Postponing decision making

There is an additional problem to do with the nature of the learning that takes place during case studies. Many students are reluctant to commit themselves to a decision. Contingency planning apparently allows the student a bolthole. It is possible to postpone the decision to some future time, however this is only an apparent refuge from decision making. In practice, contingency planning is much more complex than unconditional planning—it has to take into account all the combination of events that might occur and then define a decision in the light of those sets of circumstances. Contingency planning is not the easy way out.

This tendency to hang fire on a decision is particularly prevalent where there appears to be too little information in a case. The contingency plan then takes the form, 'do research and depending on the results follow through a particular course of action'. For example, if more than 50% of the work-force, when questioned, oppose a productivity deal, then do not go ahead with it. The problem is that research is rarely as straightforward and unequivocal as that. Suppose, for example, that in the above survey 51% of the work-force opposed the deal. Is 50% really such a clear-cut parameter on which to take two very different courses of action? Again, what about the situation where more than 50% oppose the deal but for relatively trivial reasons? With minor changes in the deal it could gain overwhelming support. Yet the contingency plan states that the deal must be dropped.

In some cases it is quite possible that the only defensible decision is to collect more information. These cases are rarer than they might at first appear but they do occur. They are relatively rare, not because most cases have a wealth of relevant information, but because in practice decisions are always taken with insufficient knowledge of the situation and the way in which it might develop. When case instructors force students to take decisions in conditions of great uncertainty they are helping to prepare them for real life decision making. As has already been pointed out, the missing information will probably be different in the case situation and in real life. However, it is the skill of making decisions under certain conditions that is being practised. The accuracy of the decision context is probably not all that important.

Collecting more information

Nevertheless, there are situations when the decision will be made to collect more information. In this case, contingency planning at some level is essential. It is simply unacceptable to call for more information without saying what it will be and how it will be collected. It is impossible to say what will be collected without knowing what decisions will be made based upon the information collected. In other words, it is still necessary to go through all the steps described in the previous chapters up to the point of evaluating alternatives. Alternatives cannot be directly evaluated in this case so the task becomes one of asking what information will help decide between them, and what values the parameters should take in order to make one decision as opposed to another. As an example, imagine the situation of an organization attempting to decide which of two product ideas to develop. It is possible to identify three major pieces of information that would be helpful in making a choice—anticipated production costs, and customer and retailer reactions to the alternative offerings. In this situation it would be expected that ways of measuring these variables would be put forward by the student. In addition, against a background of knowledge of existing product performance, it would be possible to estimate at what level a product idea must perform in order to be worthy of development, for example, production costs at least 20% less than those of existing products combined with retailer and customer preferences in a ratio of 2:1 in favour of the new product when compared with existing products. These values can be determined in advance by a process similar to that used in the evaluation step described in chapter 9. The only difference is that the evaluation produces not a choice among alternatives, e.g. product A or product B, but criteria for making that choice. The 'winning' product must be better than the 'losing' product by these margins on these important evaluation variables.

In summary, contingency planning is a powerful but rather complex technique. It should probably only be used when conditions for its use are really favourable. Some of these conditions are listed below:

(a) when the outcomes which signal different decisions are clear (e.g. a strike does or does not take place)
(b) when the outcomes are all reasonably likely to occur (there is little point in planning for a very unlikely event)
(c) when the decisions would be very different depending on the outcomes (e.g. a subsidiary would be expanded or closed down)
(d) when there is not enough information in the case on which to base a defensible decision.

11.3 GUIDE TO USE

Case students need to know when to draw the line in their analysis and how much detail to work to. This is the subject matter of section 11.1 and it is probably required reading for all new case students and may even make experienced case analysts think again about this important topic.

By contrast, section 11.2 is much less likely to be immediately useful. It does however explore some of the boundaries of the case method. Without actually using the techniques of contingency planning students may be made more aware of the continuing nature of case situations and adapt their analyses to take this more into account.

CHAPTER 12

Step Seven: Communicating Results (I)

Step seven calls for a broad-based and planned approach to the communication of case analysis results.

12.1 INTRODUCTION

I have heard students say 'I've done all the work, all I have to do now is to write it up'. This is sometimes typical of students' attitudes towards communicating the results of their analyses. It is seen as both trivial and a chore. It may be the latter, but it is certainly not the former. It is hardly any exaggeration to say that at the completion of step six you are only half way to your goal. No matter how logical, creative, exhaustive and detailed your analysis is, it counts for nothing if you fail to get it over to your audience.

A second misconception is to treat the process of communicating results in too narrow a fashion. Typically students view the process as one of 'writing a report', 'making a presentation', or 'sitting a case study examination'. What is needed, for more effective communication, is a broader framework for looking at the communication process. The one that I favour is summarized in the following widely used definition of communication:

Who says *what* to *whom* through *what channels, how,* in *what contexts,* to *what purpose* and with *what effect.*

This definition does not itself describe how to communicate effectively. It simply identifies the factors or variables which should be taken into account when making communication decisions. It can be made more helpful by structuring these factors into a four-step approach to case analysis presentation.

Step 1 Decide Aims	— to *what* purpose
Step 2 Analysis	— to *whom*
	— *who*
Step 3 Preparation and Execution	— *what*
	— *how*
Step 4 Feedback	— to *what effect*

The first step requires an answer to the question 'why communicate?'. It is concerned with the overall aims or purposes of the particular communication process you are involved in. Why you are planning to do something clearly effects *what* you intend to do and *how* you intend to do it. You might, for example, choose different content if you were trying to obtain high marks rather than to try out a new found analytical skill.

The second step is an analysis of the audience and the presenter(s). It is an analysis because, on the whole, you will have little choice in these matters. Yet understanding the audience and your fellow presenters will, or at least should, affect the content, structure and style of your presentation.

The third step, preparation and execution, is the decision-making step. The major decision will be concerned with the *what* and *how* of communication. This step is split into two stages, although these will differ in importance depending on the kind of presentation that is involved. In fact the kind of presentation will strongly affect many of the communication decisions that have to be made.

Types of presentation
You may have noticed that the factors *through what channels* and *in what contexts* do not appear in the four steps. This does not mean that they are unimportant. Their impact will be discussed but in a somewhat different way to that used for the other factors. First of all, it is useful to combine channels and contexts so that they are more specific to case presentations. The channels for case presentation are oral or written. The contexts, in broad terms, range from informal case discussion to the highly formal case examination. Combining these factors gives the four main types of presentation used for case reporting. These are:

(a) case discussions
(b) oral presentations
(c) written case analyses
(d) written case examinations

From now on the context and channel factors will be replaced by the combined factor *type of presentation*.

Type of presentation is a factor like *who* and *to whom*. It is, to a large extent, a variable outside the control of the presenter. However, it does have a very important impact on the *what* and *how* decisions. In fact the impact is so great that it really only makes sense to discuss these key decisions for each type of presentation separately. Thus step three, preparation and execution, is divided into four sections, one for each type of case presentation.

Step four involves discovering what effect a particular communication has. This is obviously important since it affects both short and long term actions. If everyone in the front row nods off to sleep in your long oral presentation, that may stimulate you to cut it short or liven it up. If your case instructor describes your writing style as too journalistic, you will want, in future written case analyses, to make it rather more formal. Step four is about feedback. In the remainder of this chapter steps one, two and four will be discussed. Step three, which requires a more detailed treatment, will be the subject of chapter 13.

12.2 DECIDE AIMS

The first and most basic question which must be answered is, 'What is this communication designed to achieve?'. Few students give this question much thought, yet activity without direction is, by definition, purposeless. There are three types of aims which you might wish to achieve when presenting a case analysis. These are educational, assessment and social. They are not only relevant to the presentation but will also affect every other aspect of case analysis. But it is in the presentation that their influence will be greatest.

12.2.1 Educational Aims

In this context this means the educational aims of the person presenting the case results. The group can be a diverse one. It includes acquiring knowledge of all kinds and at all levels, improving skills and, perhaps, even changing attitudes; in short, all the things for which the case method has been traditionally used in education.

If learning is your primary goal, this has implications for how you might expect to behave in case situations. An essential element of learning is feedback. You would probably choose to communicate in quantity both to the case instructor and fellow students. You would not have to worry too much about taking risks, but you might occasionally be made to look foolish for trying out an idea that did not work.

The goals of particular pieces of communication would determine their content. You might wish to try out a particular technique—say, financial ratio analysis. You might want to practise oral communication skills. You may wish to explore fellow students' values by concentrating discussion on the effects of redundancy on the workers during a particular case discussion. Your choice is wide though constrained, of course, by the case instructor and your fellow students.

12.2.2 Assessment Aims

The second group of purposes relates to assessment. This includes both formal assessment—the marks obtained for written case analyses, oral presentations or even participation in class discussions—as well as informal. Informal assessment may be broadly defined as what the case instructor thinks of you as a student. The two forms of assessment are often highly correlated but cause and effect are often difficult to disentangle.

The assessment objective may not necessarily be in terms of achieving good marks. You may decide that a satisficing policy of just passing courses may suit you. Nevertheless this still means a concentration on getting marks, albeit a limited amount of them.

To get good, or even adequate, marks means concentrating attention on the assessor. This, in almost all cases, is likely to be the case instructor. You will need to try to understand how to communicate to him. This is not necessarily a cynical strategy. The case instructor, in some senses, adds dynamism to the static case material. In essence he may be thought of as something of a real world substitute. He points out where students have misread or misunderstood information. He highlights errors in logic which in the real world would lead to catastrophe ('You haven't enough cash to do that!'). He evaluates recommendations by the ultimate criterion of deciding whether, in his judgement, they would be successful.

12.2.3 Social Aims

Case presentations are social situations. All of the factors which govern social behaviour come into play. In particular you are likely to have social purposes which cover such areas as status, prestige, respect and liking. You may wish to be perceived as an expert, a warm human being, a creative thinker or an excellent communicator.

Pursuing social aims leads to a variety of forms of behaviour. You may choose not to debate a point with a fellow student who you are sure is wrong but whose friendship you value. You may attempt to enhance your status by making frequent contributions which are little more than summaries of what has already been said. You may feel it is your duty to help out fellow students by allowing them to do the easiest part of a presentation. It is even possible, given enough confidence, to hand out rewards.

These, and other, examples of social behaviour occur in any group situation. They will rarely be the central concern of someone involved in making a case presentation. Nevertheless, they exist to mould and constrain behaviour, and their impact should be understood and allowed for.

12.2.4 Choosing among Aims

In practice, in most situations, you will choose a mixture of learning and assessment purposes modified and constrained by social purposes where appropriate. The balance will vary from student to student and from occasion to occasion. Of particular importance in making a decision is the ratio between learning and assessment objectives. It is possible that your learning objectives and those of your case instructor will not coincide. The case instructor has an agenda of what he wants to achieve. On average this might be fine for a whole class, but there will always be some individuals who do not agree any of the time; most of the class may not agree some of the time. Case instructors may criticize 'red herringing'. They blame students for not seeing the point of the case. This may be a symptom of conflicting learning objectives. The instructor wishes to emphasize one area of knowledge or skill, the student or students would prefer to examine another.

The tradeoff, then, is clear. If you and your instructor agree on what it is you are trying to achieve, then there is no problem. If you disagree then you must decide on the balance. How much effort should you put into doing what you want to do and how much into what your case instructor wants? It is perhaps a sad reflection of the state of education today that few students even realize that they have a choice.

Clearly the most important source of information governing the choice to be made is within yourself. 'What am I really trying to get out of this experience? How would I feel if I got really low marks?'. It is difficult to make decisions in abstract. Sometimes if you go ahead and try a particular balance between what you want and satisfying the case instructor, the tradeoffs can be seen more clearly. You can then continue to adjust as the case course proceeds.

What is important in each of these situations is not the actual mix of objectives or purposes chosen. It is the fact that a conscious choice was made from the available alternatives. You cannot begin to make a sensible communication decision until you have some notion of what it is you are trying to achieve. You may change your mind as the course proceeds: that is to be expected. What is important is that a coherent set of explicit and well-considered purposes, and means of achieving them, should have been worked out.

12.3 ANALYSIS—TO WHOM

Perhaps the most common piece of advice given in books on report writing is, 'Write for your audience'. This seems obvious, almost trite. It is easy to convince people that it is an excellent principle to follow. After all, communication is not complete until it is received. The audience is obviously the target to be aimed at and must be kept in mind.

12.3.1 Audiences and their Characteristics

The audience or audiences depends upon the type of presentation. A written case analysis or examination will normally only be seen by the case instructor. An oral presentation or case discussion will involve both the case instructor and fellow students.

These two audiences differ in terms of two important characteristics: (a) knowledge/skills and (b) motivation for attending to a communication from a presenter.

Knowledge

There is clearly a major difference in the level of knowledge and skill between case instructors and the students they teach. At the lowest level this means, for example, that the case instructor knows the facts of the case better. The instructor will also know what problems are likely to emerge in discussion, what solutions will be proposed, and which is likely to emerge as the 'best'. This will be even clearer if the case instructor has taught the case before. At a higher level, the instructor should be expected to have a wider grasp of the discipline being taught. He should also be more skilled in the arts of communication—both receiving and sending. In short, the case instructor is a professional and the students are, as yet, amateurs.

Motivation

The second characteristic of importance is motivation. The case instructor will have a number of objectives in mind when reading a case analysis or listening to a case discussion. He will probably be attempting to assess individual students. He will need to be attentive, especially in case discussions. He will weigh contributions from a number of angles; how logical they are; how they build upon other contributions; how creative they are, and so on. These are very complex judgements. The case instructor will also be looking beyond assessment of the individual student. He will be gathering evidence about the quantity and quality of learning going on. He may be looking, in a case discussion, to redirecting students' attention. In reading written case analyses he may be drawing conclusions about how to run the next session.

One final point about the case instructor is worth making. Having done a case several times, a case instructor may come to know it too well. He may, for example, fail to recognize a new and original approach. In a limited sense, he may be said to have a closed mind.

Fellow students

Students really only form an audience for case communications in class discussion. In this situation they form an audience with rather different characteristics from those of the case instructor. Frequently they have not fully mastered the facts in the case. A particular situation may come as a complete surprise because they failed to see a footnote or interpret a table correctly. Unlike the case instructor, they may have tackled the case in only one way. A different approach might find them completely at sea, particularly if it involves the use of complex, analytical techniques or convoluted arguments. They are not fully familiar with the concepts and techniques of the discipline. This means that a simple statement may be miscommunicated because students are still trying to remember what a particular Act of Parliament said. The motivations of students also differ from those of the case instructor. Students, as discussed in the last section, will wish to learn and gain good assessment. They may or may not believe that they will learn much by listening to their colleagues.

In summary, then, the case instructor can be viewed as an expert and interested listener but with definite ideas about what the case is all about. Fellow students form an inexpert and diverse audience concerned with their own problems of understanding and making good impressions on the case instructor and each other.

12.3.2 Choice of Audience

In fact, at the most general level, there is very little choice to be made. Written analyses are read only by the case instructor. Even in oral presentation or case discussions there would be little point in addressing one audience to the exclusion of the other. However, because of the heterogeneity of the audience in the latter case a subsidiary choice must be made. This is the decision concerning 'at what level to pitch the communication'. Pitch it at too high a level and you will lose the less intelligent or ill-prepared student. Pitch it at too low a level and you risk giving the wrong impression to the case instructor.

It is always possible, of course, to adopt a mixed strategy. This means aiming some of the communications at one audience and some at the other. This is not too difficult to do in a free form case discussion. Since contributions are likely to be discrete and to some extent unrelated, they can be aimed in different directions without too much worry about their being inconsistent. However, in a formal case presentation this is more difficult. It implies a simple structure for the least well-equipped students to follow with occasional more detailed and complex asides for the case instructor. A mixed strategy is not an easy form of communication to master, but it may be the only solution in some instances.

12.3.3 Researching Audiences

The primary source of information will be classroom behaviour. You will need to analyse not only the content of what goes on in class, but also the process. How does what is said reveal things about the speakers? It may be that the class is short on quantitative expertise and shuns any analysis of this kind. They may value experience and example rather than theory. They may not be doing the reading specified as essential to the case course. The case instructor may be particularly keen on creative and unusual solutions. He may appear to be weak on the accounting side. He may never direct questions to students by name. Data like these are useful in building up a picture of the key characteristics of your potential audiences. These data will become more numerous as the course proceeds. In theory, therefore, you should have developed quite a reasonable understanding of your audiences, which in turn means that you must consider adapting your plans to fit in with the changing picture.

12.3.4 Reaching Audiences

Having identified and understood your audiences, the next step is to remember to prepare your communication with these audiences very much in your mind. This principle is all too easily forgotten in practice. You will find it only too easy to disappear into a world of your own making. You may finish up talking to yourself and be surprised when your audience does not understand. You will often fail to step back from what you are doing to take a broader view. This piece of advice bears repeating any number of times. Keep the audience constantly in mind. Even more specifically, imagine a particular person (or two or three) in the target audience, hearing or reading what you plan to communicate. What would their reaction be? Would they understand all the terms used? Will they be able to follow the line of argument? Would it run counter to any of their current attitudes or values? Would it be within their range of experience? Questions like these serve to keep feet well and truly on the ground.

12.4 ANALYSIS—WHO

The characteristic of the person or people delivering a message will obviously have a major impact on the communication process. Two dissimilar presenters making the same speech will have different effects on an audience. Understanding the influence a 'sender' may have is essential if the message is to be transmitted effectively. The situation becomes even more complex when the presentation is prepared and executed by a group.

12.4.1 Individual Presentations

The *who* effect should not be confused with the *how* or *what* effects. The class quantitative methods expert could present an inaccurate and inappropriate piece of statistical analysis. Since the source has credibility people are more likely to question their own understanding rather than the expertise of the presenter. The message is given a particular value because of who is delivering it as well as how it is being delivered and what is being said.

There are a number of different dimensions along which an audience can assess a communicator. These include intellectual abilities and skills, attitudes and personality characteristics, as well as how knowledgeable and experienced an individual is judged to be. Clearly these are all perceptions that an audience may have. They may not necessarily coincide with your own views of yourself. Nevertheless since the audience's perceptions will affect the way in which a message is received, it is their views which must be understood and taken into account.

Your first task will be to try, as honestly as you can, to judge what your audience thinks about you. It might be worthwhile to write a short pen portrait of yourself as seen through others' eyes. Think back over your past experience in class and ask yourself how you may have appeared to others. It may even be worth discussing it with friends.

The second task is to make sure that you work within the perceptions that others have of you. If you don't, you will simply not be credible. It is futile for an 18 year old to use phrases like 'In my experience of industry . . .'. If you failed the accountancy examinations, few of the people who know this are going to take your breakeven analysis seriously. A student who has consistently argued that 'money is the only motivator' can hardly be expected to be believed when he recommends a 'job enrichment programme' in a case presentation. The key question to ask is, 'Will they believe this coming from me?'.

It is important not to exaggerate the source effect in communications. An audience can change its view of a presenter because of the presentation. In many case presentations the audience will know very little about the presenter. On the other hand it is important that the source and the message reinforce rather than contradict one another. Since the source is fixed, the message, or at least how it is presented, must be adapted.

12.4.2 Group Presentations

Oral or written group presentations are quite common in case courses. They present a number of additional presentation problems as well as some worthwhile opportunities. What one should look for are ways of exploiting the opportunities while avoiding the most obvious pitfalls.

Group work should be more creative, effective and fun. Greater creativity stems not only from a larger pool of ideas, but also from the fact that one person will 'spark off' another to produce even more brilliant ideas. Increased effectiveness should result from simple division of labour. If each member of a group is given part of the whole task to perform then the whole analysis can be completed very much more quickly. Working together, for most people most of the time, is more enjoyable than working apart. When motivation is hard to maintain, the discipline and enjoyment inherent in group work is often crucial.

Group problems

The major problem of group work is harnessing the resources of the group to achieve specific ends. Creativity is of little use if the results are not used. Division of labour is a waste of time if the tasks do not dovetail together to produce a coherent whole. There is little enjoyment in working in a group which is divided and fractious.

To avoid these problems it is necessary to build and maintain an organization to carry out the necessary tasks. Coordination of effort is the main requirement and the traditional methods of coordination involve rules and roles. The trick is to ensure that these guide, but do not constrain the group's efforts. The first order of business might be simply to decide what rules and roles will apply.

Rules and roles

Rules could cover such things as when and where meetings are to be held, how long they will normally be, what members should have done before the meeting, how work is to be allocated, etc. Roles could cover both administrative (chairman, secretary) and specialist (accountant, mathematician) functions. On the whole I favour administrative roles. Their function will be to see that the machinery operates relatively smoothly. They will be concerned with process rather than content. Specialists are less easy to justify. Case analyses require complex tasks to be performed. It is difficult in the first place to cut the whole up into meaningful parts. It is even more difficult to put those parts back together into a coherent and sensible whole. That is not to say that specific and well defined tasks cannot be delegated, e.g., 'Joe, could you look up the wording of the relevant Act before next time?'. But asking Clive to 'look after' marketing, Vera to take care of production and Dennis to watch over accounting simply will not work in most situations. In other words, most people should do most things. This means that the group may be less efficient but it is better coordinated.

Cooperation and conflict

Cooperation rather than conflict should be the order of the day. However, this cannot be left to chance. Cooperation is more likely if people like each other. Thus time spent 'horsing around' should not be begrudged. It not only provides rewards for the individual but also helps to build relationships. It is time spent maintaining the machinery. Conflicts will however arise on occasions. These are better dealt with by preset rules rather than by continuing acrimonious debate. For example, it may be agreed that all major differences will be resolved by voting or that individuals disagreeing with a particular approach may disengage from tasks associated with it. Groups can also enhance their performance by spending some time discussing how they are working. Again this should be seen as a legitimate use of the group's time and not as idle navel-gazing. Practical suggestions, 'Why don't we split into two groups to discuss the two main issues?', should be the order of the day. Character assassination should be avoided at all cost!

Much of what has been discussed so far relates to the initial phases of the analysis. But in the final analysis a written report or an oral presentation is required. How should groups handle this final phase of their task?

Written group presentations

For a written presentation the sequence of events might follow this sort of order. An initial meeting would discuss the case in general terms perhaps using the step by step approach described in this book. Gaps in analysis or information may be recognized and individuals would be asked to fill those gaps. A second meeting might move quite close to providing an overall structure, and even some of the detail, for a first draft. This first draft should then be written by a single individual. While this means a lot of work for one individual, the alternative is even less desirable. A number of individuals could write separate sections. This would almost certainly mean having to attempt a major rewrite in committee. This is almost impossible to do with any efficiency. A single unified draft can, however, be amended within the group. A second draft might be necessary but this could be the work of another individual. The important point is that strategy and minor amendments should be done in the group; writing should be done outside the group.

Oral group presentations

An oral presentation would probably benefit from taking a similar sequence. However, the final draft in this case is not a report but something approaching a script. Again one individual should be responsible for putting into words the group's agreed position. In addition to amendments to the script structure the group would also have to be responsible for designing the visual aids to go with the presentation. At this point the group can opt for an individual or group presentation. If an individual is presenting then the script structure is handed over to that individual to flesh out in a way that fits his own personal delivery. However, the least the other members of the group can do is to be an audience for his rehearsals and provide useful and constructive feedback.

If more than one member of the group is to present then some additional decisions have to be made. How will the presentation be split up? Natural breaks will exist within the flow of the presentation and these should be used as points at which to pass over the presentation. Links must be written so that handover is as smooth as possible, and the structure can be described in personal as well as content terms. ('I'm starting off with a look at some of the major problems the organization has. I'll then hand over to Harry who will . . . and finally Wendy will pull it all together at the end and summarize what we have all said.') Within each section each presenter should be allowed to use his own presentation style as long as it fits within the structure he has been asked to use. Presenters should not read from prepared scripts. This is very difficult to do well. In addition different presentation styles offer variety and interest. The message should, however, remain clear beneath the different treatments.

Finally the whole presentation must be well rehearsed. The handovers must be done quickly and smoothly if they are not to be disruptive. Visual aids must be carefully planned so that delays are not created as each new presenter arranges his material. Rehearsal breeds confidence which is very necessary when the complexities of a group presentation are being attempted. Doing case analyses in group settings provides opportunities as well as posing problems. A theme which has been played so many times in this book deserves repetition here. You should be aware of what alternatives are available to you and make conscious, clearly thought out decisions rather than be driven by events.

12.5 FEEDBACK—TO WHAT EFFECT

Although feedback is the last step in the four-step sequence of communication, its placement here can be justified. Feedback can occur before, during and after communication. It also requires some thought and planning before the event if it is to be captured and used to improve your performance. Understanding the timing, level, sources and kinds of feedback help in this planning process.

12.5.1 Timing and Level of Feedback

Feedback can occur before, during and after some types of case presentation. In particular it is possible to rehearse an oral presentation in front of a sympathetic audience, watch for reaction during the actual presentation and ask for the case instructor's reaction afterwards. In principle the earlier and greater the feedback the better your performance is likely to be. This suggests rehearsals or getting someone to read through a written analysis or asking your case instructor to mark 'mock' case examination answers. All of these examples imply that there is one major piece of communication for which you have to prepare. Therefore there are situations in which supplementary feedback is possible and indeed valuable.

Not all feedback occurs at the same level. To take two extremes: you may note the effect on an audience of slowing an oral presentation or you may ask your case instructor how your case analysis skills are developing. These are at very different levels of generality. The more general the level of feedback the more information you must expect to collect.

12.5.2 Sources and Kinds of Feedback

Feedback comes mostly from people: fellow students, the case instructor, friends and, paradoxically, yourself. You can listen to or read your own words, and a salutary experience this can be. Communicators are often so busy thinking about what they are going to say or write that they ignore what they have just said or written. But the shortest, and therefore very powerful, feedback loops are between the lips and the ears, the pen and the eyes. In short, be aware of what and how you are communicating while you are doing it.

In practice, though, you will mostly rely on your audience for feedback. Some of this will be solicited, some unsolicited. Unsolicited feedback comprises all those messages which your audience sends back to you unasked for. For example, someone may ask a question during an oral presentation which indicates that you have not got over your point. Of course feedback can be non-verbal as well as verbal. Yawns, raised eyebrows or rapt attention can provide you with very good indications of what effect your communication is having.

Unsolicited feedback is direct and open but may not be very revealing. Sometimes it is necessary to go behind the immediate reaction and ask people how they react to what you have communicated. Case instructors provide this kind of feedback routinely for written case analyses and oral presentations but will not, unless specially asked, comment on how you have performed in a class discussion or case examination. Fellow students may be prepared to discuss your performances or comment on written work before it is handed in. However, you should be aware of the burden you are placing on them and use this resource sparingly. Friends, acting as audiences for oral or written presentations before the event, may also be asked what the communication problems are and how they might be resolved. Tape-recording rehearsals, or, with permission, the classroom presentation, provides another and more permanent form of feedback.

12.5.3 What Feedback to Collect

If you are planning to collect feedback you must decide not only how you are going to collect it but also what you are going to collect. Primarily this should be determined by your communication aims. If you are concerned to improve your oral skills then feedback concerning your speaking performance is required. If you are not sure that you understand the application of a particular technique you may ask the case instructor to comment on how you applied it in a particular written case analysis. Such an approach means looking ahead to the actual communication situation and deciding what feedback you are going to collect and how you are going to do it. It is usually worth, as a matter of discipline, committing these plans to paper.

Often the most valuable bits of feedback occur unexpectedly and are unplanned. You may suddenly realize that you have been spelling a word incorrectly since primary school or that you have misunderstood a basic psychological concept. This means that when you are communicating you should be as receptive as you can to all kinds and forms of feedback, which is easy advice to give but difficult to carry out: it requires an attitude change more than anything else. Remembering that communication is a two-way process is a good start.

You may learn not only from your own actions but also from those of others. Vicarious learning can be a very powerful experience. This is particularly true when someone is doing something wrong rather than right. Watch how others perform and write, and see how the audience, including you, reacts. Educational opportunities abound if only one could take advantage of them.

CHAPTER 13

Step Seven:
Communicating Results (II)

13.1 INTRODUCTION

In this chapter the preparation and execution of the communication of case results will be discussed. This will be done separately for each of the four major types of case presentation—case discussions, oral presentations, written case analyses and case examinations. It was argued in the last chapter that these contexts are really so different that they require separate consideration. That is not to suggest that certain principles do not apply to them all. They do, but their application in each context is sufficiently different to make separate treatment easier to understand.

13.2 CASE DISCUSSION

Case discussions are the least structured context for communicating the results of case analyses. The amount of structure is largely at the case instructor's discretion. At one end of the spectrum some choose to adopt a minimum interference strategy. At the other end instructors can set particular questions to answer, or structure the discussion by prompting and questioning. Even in this situation however a considerable amount of freedom exists.

This freedom often makes case discussion seem confused and chaotic. It is difficult to present long and complex arguments orally. Fellow students interrupt to make their own points. Arguments are simplified and this leads to misunderstandings. Contributions cannot be planned in detail, so they are sometimes badly presented and fail to communicate. Because analysis and communication are occurring at the same time, students miss whole chunks of discussion and points have to be repeated. Frequently the discussion cycles, apparently endlessly, around a series of central issues. Occasionally it will switch abruptly to another task. In summary, the content and presentation of contributions are made under difficult conditions and this must be recognized in preparing a case for discussion.

13.2.1 Case Discussion—Preparation

Most of the preparation for a classroom discussion has to do with content. By the very nature of the situation 'what you say' and 'how you say it' decisions will be made on the spot, in the classroom. Likewise it is clear that practising presentation of points to be made during a classroom discussion will not be a very effective use of time: prepared speeches rarely find a place in the case debate. However, there are ways in which points can be prepared, in outline, so that they are more likely to be well received.

Organization

The major priority in preparing for a case discussion is organization. At the lowest level this means organizing and indexing your notes so that you know where everything is. You must be able to find the relevant material in the heat of debate. If there is little structure imposed by the case instructor then it is important to create a system that allows you quick and easy access to the work you have done. Since the discussion can go in any direction you must be able to flip a few pages and remind yourself what you decided about a particular piece of information, solution, or outcome. It is particularly important to keep track of analysis you might have thought unimportant or solutions you rejected. Since the discussion can follow any track, they might actually turn out to be rather important. If the case instructor imposes a predictable structure on the discussion, then your material organization should reflect that structure. If, for example, he always asks the same lead-off question, you should prepare an answer to it culled from your rough notes. If the sequence of the discussion is always the same, then organize along parallel lines.

The process of organizing the material helps you achieve another important task, that of memorizing the key aspects of the case and your analysis of it. The balance between memory and notes is an individual decision. Most students rely too heavily on memory, rather assuming that they will not be able to use their notes efficiently in class. This is a fallacy and a dangerous one. It often means that the level of discussion stays at a more superficial level than it would have done had the students organized their notes to make them more easily accessible.

'Points'

At a more detailed level, it is important to summarize and clarify your results by means of 'points'. The point is probably the most useful unit of presentation in a classroom discussion. It recognizes the difficulty of sustaining long and complex arguments. A point essentially summarizes a part of your analysis and might look like this.

There are three major solutions and two minor ones

(a)　close the plant
(b)　reorganize it
　　　(i)　into divisions
　　　(ii) by unions
(c)　expand it

These points do not stand alone. They will usually be related in what one might call arguments. Here are four points which form part of an argument.

(a)　The factory has been losing money for the last three years.
(b)　The cash flow position of the group (analysis of appendix 3) has recently taken a turn for the worse.
(c)　The order book (table 6.4) looks good for the next three months but deteriorates rapidly thereafter.
(d)　In about six months there will be tremendous financial pressure from the group to close the factory.

It might just be possible to get all these points across at one go, but it is more likely that after one point has been made, other people will make the others and it will be left to you to sum up with the last point.

These points are obviously organized within the structure you have chosen to use. They simply represent the best and most succinct summary you can provide, in convenient units, of the analyses you have carried out. They provide a springboard for the oral contributions you wish to make. They should therefore be written in such a way as to make them easy to get across. This does not mean writing out small prepared speeches. It does mean trying to figure out how best you might get over a particular point.

Getting over points
There are a number of ways in which this might be done. A diagram or matrix written on the blackboard might be a very effective way of getting over a complex point. You will obviously have to prepare this beforehand and be prepared to capture the blackboard during the discussion. Lists are useful. ('I think there are three reasons why the company should go ahead with this.') If a point comes from an exhibit, it pays to stop the discussion so that everyone has access to it before you start your explanation. ('If we can all look at table 5.3 on page 6, production capacity is given here as 1500 tonnes . . .') Relating the point to a familiar concept or experience also helps. ('There seems to be a prime example of cognitive dissonance in this case. When the chief accountant decided . . .'. Or, 'This is exactly the same problem that British Leyland is facing now. The product line is . . .') You are simply trying to find 'hooks' upon

which to hang key points so that they can be more readily understood.

13.2.2 Case Discussion—Execution

One of the important options that you have in a classroom discussion is what role or roles to assume. Few students realize that they have a choice. There are two main types of role, content roles and process roles. Content roles are those where individuals lay claim to being experts in terms of some parts of the content of a case. Process roles are those roles which affect the structure and the flow of the case discussion almost without regard to the content. The benefits from students taking roles are two-fold. It gives the individual a clearer view of what he should be doing within the case discussion. It also helps to improve the quality of case discussions by ensuring that certain specialist functions are being carried out. This adds width and shape to the discussion. If the roles are all filled or if you feel that the benefits of taking a role do not exceed the costs—in terms of the extra effort required—then your decision may be not to take a role.

Content roles

Content roles all revolve around the concept of an expert. An individual taking such a role signals by his classroom behaviour his readiness to act as an authority on one aspect of the case. ('I've spent a lot of time analysing the accounting data in this case.') The expertise can be along a number of dimensions. These include techniques (accounting, quantitative, etc.), experience (general or specific to the case), description (marketing, production, psychology), stage of analysis (analytic, creative, evaluative) or even one particular aspect of the case. What the expert says in essence is, 'I have studied the case in one particular way and here are my insights which I expect will be useful.'. Experts add breadth to the discussion of a case. There is, however, a risk, from their point of view, that they do so at some personal risk. If an expert concentrates on one line of attack, then his own viewpoint will necessarily be rather narrow. It is a mistake, I believe, to let an expert role dominate the way a case is analysed. The expert role is a communications role and should be assumed after a more general analysis has been completed.

Process roles

In contrast, process roles require little preparation, and switching roles is much more likely to occur. Process roles are those roles which help support and develop the process of discussion. A number of such roles have been identified, but the list is far from complete.

The 'librarian's' role is to ensure that no data is overlooked in any discussion. He keeps pointing out relevant paragraphs, exhibits and appendices without necessarily progressing the discussion any further. The role is rather limited in scope, but in the early days of a case course it can be a very useful one.

The 'questioner's' role is to add depth and clarity to the discussion. Clarity is added through questions like, 'Sorry, Brian, I didn't understand that. Could you go through that again?'. Depth is obtained through questions like, 'But why do you think management would go for the redundancy rather than the redeployment option?'. This is a delicate role to play. Fellow students are apt to believe that asking questions is easier than answering them and that the questioner is taking the easy option. Case instructors may feel that their role is being usurped. It is a role to be taken sparingly and perhaps interspersed with the taking of other roles.

The 'integrator's' role is to weave together the strands of the discussion and to make something out of them. An integrator goes beyond what is said. ('If George's cost analysis is correct and if we assume that the forecasts in table 1 are OK, then the product has to be a winner.') An integrator is particularly useful in the first few cases, in very complex cases, or when the general level of preparation is low. These are all situations where more analysis is going on inside the classroom than outside it. An integrator will usually have had to do fairly intensive preparation.

The 'controller's' role is perhaps the most demanding role of all. In a sense it is the role that the case instructor would play if he wished to adopt an interventionalist role. Controlling the discussion means a number of things. It means ensuring that most of the major topics are actually covered. It means ensuring that all topics are covered in depth. It means controlling interruptions and red herrings. It may also mean acting as a referee when the discussion gets rather too heated for comfort. All of these interventions require social skills of a high order. Done well this role can be enormously rewarding to the individual and the group. Done badly it can prove disastrous.

Involvement

In addition to specific role behaviour some comments might be usefully made about general case discussion behaviour. One of the most important decisions to be made concerns level of involvement. Students raised in the English education tradition tend to be diffident and self-effacing. They are taught not to push themselves forward or offer opinions unless directly asked. Clearly this is highly limiting in a case discussion. In general, my advice would be to get more involved than you feel comfortable with. However, this level of involvement has to be carefully monitored. It is all too easy for the rest of the class to relax in the certain knowledge that one or two individuals will make the running. It therefore pays to break up the pattern occasionally.

Listening

The counterpoint to contributing is listening. Few of us are very adept at this essential skill. In a case discussion it is all too easy to let the mind wander. Sometimes shutting out the discussion is necessary in order to think through something; at other times it is all too easy to suffer lapses of concentration. To get the most out of case discussions requires effort. The greatest effort is that of concentrating on what is being said and what it means. One major aid to listening and understanding is to map out the shape of the discussion. You may even want to do this on a piece of paper just to remind yourself of what has been said. Any new contribution can then be related to what has gone before. It is still not an easy task to listen and concentrate. Nevertheless, it is a central social skill in management and therefore one to be developed by as much practice as possible.

Attitude to Fellow students

Another general area of case discussion decisions relates to your behaviour towards fellow students. In general you should try to maintain attitudes of respect, constructiveness, open-mindedness and support. This is more a statement about learning than morality. Your fellow students represent a major source of new learning for you. Evaluate the contribution, not its source or the way in which it was presented. Similarly, if you respect and support your fellow students you are creating a richer learning situation. Everyone will feel free to contribute without fear of attack. This does not mean that debate should not take place, but the counter position should be carefully and unemotionally stated. Not 'That's a stupid idea' but 'I see what you're getting at but isn't there a fairly major problem?'.

Helping the discussion

A number of positive ways in which you can help the discussion along have already been mentioned. Don't keep repeating your contributions. It is true that not everyone will have taken them in first time. However, those who have will not thank you for harping back on the same theme. If you feel it is absolutely necessary to do so, try a fresh approach and only introduce the idea again when it is relevant. Try to distinguish between controlled developments of the discussion and red herrings. If you feel that a particular topic has been exhausted, say so and introduce a new one with an original contribution. It is up to the rest of the class to decide whether to follow. Don't throw in the brilliant, but irrelevant, idea you have just had. Wait until the time is ripe and it becomes a relevant issue. In these and other ways you should see it as part of your task to keep the discussion effective and interesting. To do so may mean subjugating your own needs to those of the group. Practice in this process is no bad thing, however.

Simplicity, clarity, precision

Oral presentation of a contribution should be governed by the knowledge that it will be a transitory communication, difficult to follow and remember. The point should therefore be simple, clear, and as precise as possible. If you can add a simple structure ('I have two points to make'), so much the better. Try to avoid hedging bets and qualifying statements like this: 'I believe that, other things being equal, on the whole, taking everything into consideration, the product could, given the right conditions, be a qualified success'. The statement, 'This product will succeed' is more interesting and much easier to understand, and a statement like this will produce discussion as well as make an immediate and easily understood impact. The qualifications can emerge in the subsequent discussion. It is not necessary to make every statement self-contained and watertight. Attempting to do so results in stilted and long-winded discussions.

Case discussions provide an excellent example of the old adage 'You only get out what you put in'. It is not difficult to 'hide' throughout a course which relies on discussion in a large student group, but the educational opportunity cost is very great. You can learn a great deal and develop skills quickly in the hothouse atmosphere of case discussions. It would be a pity to throw that chance away.

13.3 ORAL PRESENTATIONS

Oral presentations generally involve an individual, sometimes a group, taking most of a teaching period to deliver the results of a case analysis, often with visual aids. The rest of the class and the case instructor form the audience. Oral presentations are in many ways easier to plan for than classroom discussions. The structure of the discussion is under your control since you, or a member of your group, will be the only one speaking. This means that the emphasis moves from the execution to the preparation phase.

13.3.1 Oral Presentations—Preparation

Problems

Oral communications are essentially transitory in nature. They are delivered and then only partially heard or remembered. They are forgotten because it is impossible for most individuals to remember a long speech word for word. Only key points are remembered. In addition these key points will vary from individual to individual, they may not be the key points the presenter would have liked to be remembered, or indeed they may not be the actual points made. The transience of oral communication gives rise to five problems which you must be aware of and do your best to avoid when planning a presentation.

(a)   First of all there is the problem of delivering the message. Written communications can be reviewed and rewritten by the author before giving them to an audience. This is not possible, at least to the same degree, when speaking. Who has not had that sinking feeling that there is no way to finish the sentence and still make sense? The act of speaking requires planning ahead. It is very difficult to do this and assess what one has just said.

(b)   If delivery of oral communications is difficult, listening is no less easy a task. An audience can re-read a written sentence or passage that they have failed to understand at the first pass. This luxury is not available in oral communication. The usual process is that the listener repeats the sentence which he has retained in short-term memory. This usually means that the next sentence or two is missed. The thread of the argument is broken. The listener struggles to catch up and misses or mishears much of what is said. He often gives up, returning to the fray at an obvious re-entry point, e.g. 'And now my third point'.

(c)   Comprehension is a short-term communication goal. But what of the longer term? Without mechanical storage much of what is said will be quickly forgotten. Most human minds have a rather limited storage capacity. If what is being said now must be related to something that was said much earlier, it may be based upon very shaky foundations. Audiences need to be given these foundations in some permanent form so that they can always relate to them. They need structure.

(d)   A related point has to do with the absolute memory capacity of an audience. This is usually much less than one thinks: it is easy to over-estimate it. A presenter is, or should be, thoroughly familiar with the material. It is therefore difficult to judge how much members of an audience can take when they are presented with a wealth of new material for the first time. In their eagerness to communicate their productivity, student presenters frequently overload their audiences.

(e)   The converse of this problem is that students often under-estimate the time required for a presentation. They find themselves under pressure and in their haste they attempt to get a quart into a pint pot. The results are seldom edifying.

Opportunities

Much has been made of the problems of oral communication. However, it does have two important advantages.

(a) Oral presentations can be very compelling; much more so than the written word. The presence of a living, talking human being, especially if he radiates interest and enthusiasm, is difficult to ignore. Attitude and emotion can add tremendously to the impact of a message.

(b) Oral presentations also have the capacity, though it is used less often than it might be, to be flexible. Presenters can respond to the changing environment, human, physical, or temporal. They can also adapt their style, and even their material, as they sense the mood of an audience. This is a rather skilled accomplishment. Nevertheless, it is one which can be practised in everyday life, in conversation. It is also a very necessary skill for organizational survival.

Information

More specific information is required before you begin to prepare your presentation. The importance of knowing your audience has already been discussed in section 12.3.1. You must also find out what the case instructor's ground rules are. These may include length of presentation, structure and availability of resources such as overhead projectors, flip charts, etc. You may also want to find out what is negotiable. If you can make a good case for doing something different you will be listened to. If you just go ahead and do it the chances are you will be penalized.

Structure

Structure is of paramount importance in an oral presentation. This is due to the transitory nature of oral communication as discussed earlier. In order for the audience to comprehend and remember the content a clear structure must be used and must be seen to be used. No single structure works best in all situations. Some alternatives are given in table 13.1. These are only three of the alternative general purpose structures that could be used for an oral presentation. The elements are not very different: some are at a more general level than others, but the major difference lies in the sequence. Broadly there appear to be two alternatives —top down or bottom up. The top down approach presents the solution first, as in Alternative 1, and then justifies that solution. The bottom up approach starts with the problems and reveals the solution at the end. Both have their merits. The top down approach engages interest at the beginning but is difficult to present logically. The bottom up approach follows a clear sequence but can prove long winded and boring.

Other more original structures are possible, and their creation and use is to be encouraged, but the audience should be left in no doubt about what the structure means and how it works. If the skeleton does not hang together the flesh can never be put on the bones. An outline of the structure of the presentation will therefore usually form an early part of your speech. It is said that a tip for any instructors goes as follows:

Tell them what you are going to tell them
Tell them
Tell them what you told them

This is not bad advice. It establishes structure early on and reinforces it with a recapitulation at the end.

Simplicity

Simplicity is also important in communicating structure. Probably fewer than 10 headings will suffice. Any more than this and the audience will not be able to keep the whole shape of the presentation in mind. The headings should also be simple and almost self-explanatory. In any case, when outlining the structure of the presentation they should be explained in somewhat more detail.

'In the section on alternatives I will outline the four major alternatives I see that the organization has, and what I expect might result from implementing each.'

Alternative 1	Alternative 2	Alternative 3
Recommendations	Attention-getter outline	Outline
Why these	Background	Conclusions
Why not others	Problem statement	Problems
Supporting evidence	Alternatives and analysis	Alternatives
	Implementation plan	Criteria for choice
	Restatement of	Action plan
	problems/solutions	Recapitulation
	What must be done/	
	benefits	
	Questions	

Table 13.1 Alternative Structures for Oral Presentations

One important structural variable that has already been discussed is length. In general you will be working to a time limit. It is worthwhile to allocate that time among the elements of the structure you choose to adopt. This helps to control the natural inclination to try to cover too much ground. It is better to have this discipline early so that the presentation remains in some sort of time balance.

Sequence has already been mentioned as an important aspect of structure. A clear story line must be present at each level of the presentation. Thus it is important to structure the sequence within a segment as well as the overall sequence of the segments. For example:

'For each alternative I am going to look at the cash flow, the organization and the Chemical Products Division.'

To achieve continuity of the story line the best approach is to start at the most general level and work down until the right level of detail is reached. This ensures that the whole presentation is consistent, a very important attribute for any communication. An example of working down is given below.

Problem Statement
Major Problems 1.1   Statement
               1.2   Symptoms
                      1.2.1 Cash flow (historic, forecast)
                      1.2.2 Ratios
               2.1   Statement
               2.2   Symptoms
                      2.2.1 Chairman's statement
                      2.2.2 Appendix III analysis
                      2.2.3 Graph 1
               3.1   Statement
               3.2   Symptoms
                      3.2.1 Marketing manager's job description
                      3.2.2 Share of advertising figures
                      3.2.3 Chairman's statement
                      3.2.4 Exhibits 1 to 3

Although structure must be described orally, this is not really sufficient. An audience cannot hold a structure in its short-term memory having only heard it once. It is, I believe, essential in any oral presentation to have the structure displayed in writing throughout. This can then be referred to by the audience at any time, not just when changing segments. The presenter can easily refer to the structure at any time, either to remind people of the point the presentation has reached or to refer back or forward to other segments.

In summary, the structure of an oral presentation should be simple, compact, logical, self-explanatory and available at all times to the audience.

Level of Detail

As a rule presenters give too much rather than too little detail in oral presentations. They seem to want to demonstrate their productivity or else heavily buttress their position with data. But in an oral presentation detail cannot be comprehended: it adds enormously to the length of the presentation and it camouflages the main themes and arguments. In particular it is important not to include a long recital of details already available in the case as 'background'. If the audience is fully prepared this is redundant, while if it is not it will never be able to grasp the details sufficiently well to make sense of what follows.

Visual Aids

What visual aids you use and how you use them should be decisions you make early on in your planning. Often they are considered only at the last moment. This means that they are badly executed and not integrated with the rest of the presentation. Nor is it effective simply to write out ˹lmost everything you are going to say on a flip chart or overhead projector slide. Visual aids should only be used when they add to the effectiveness of a presentation in one of the following ways:

(a) To help the audience remember the structure of the whole presentation

(b) To provide the audience with the structure of a section within the overall presentation

(c) To emphasize key points clearly and dramatically (photographs, diagrams, graphs)

(d) To show unavoidable detail

(e) To demonstrate the internal workings of a complex argument or calculation

(f) To break up a long section of speech

In visual terms, the main fault with visual aids is to try to get too much on one slide or blackboard at a time. Too much visual information is confusing and lacks impact. If in doubt, put less on each slide and use more slides.

Different visual aids have different characteristics. Blackboards and handouts both suffer from a major disadvantage. Since visual aids have to be prepared, the whole of the written side of the presentation is available to the audience before a word is spoken. This is distracting at the beginning of a presentation when the audience proceeds to glance through or over the material. It also leads to boredom and frustration because people know exactly what is coming and are longing for the presenter to get on with it. Flipcharts and other paper presentation methods are usually good and relatively inexpensive. They are, however, somewhat difficult to use smoothly in the middle of a presentation. Projector slides are difficult and expensive to prepare, though they are of very high visual quality. However, the best medium for most oral presentations is the overhead projector slide. These can be prepared in colour, are easy to handle, have good visual qualities, and can be altered in the middle of a presentation. Preparation has been made much simpler by the development of processes which can convert images on paper to transparencies.

Repetition

Oral information is difficult to grasp. Repetition is one solution to this problem. It has to be used carefully, however. Too much repetition is boring. Only key points bear repetition. One example of this is reminding the audience of the structure ('And now I want to move on to the third section and talk about the problems as I see them.'). Another is the summary or recapitulation of the presentation that is given at the end. ('To summarize, I think that Smith Ltd. should build the new factory for these key reasons.') A third example might be a point that needs to be fully understood. ('Let me repeat that this forecast is based on the assumption that there is no economic recession in the UK during the next five years.') Repetitions need not appear repetitious: saying the same thing in a different way helps to add variety to the presentation while still achieving the objective of reinforcement.

Planning delivery

The most important issue concerning the planning of what you are actually going to say is the level of preparation. The alternatives are to read from a prepared text or to speak from brief notes. Few experienced teachers would recommend the former to beginning presenters. In the first place, it is very difficult to write a speech which will sound spontaneous and interesting. In the second, it is very difficult to deliver such a speech effectively. Some politicians never seem to manage it! The written and spoken words are very different: successfully transforming one form to another is a very difficult communication task and is best avoided.

Thus there are strong arguments for adopting a more flexible, less structured approach. Having worked out the structure and content of your presentation, the next step is to convert them into a 'bridge' which will carry you easily and effectively into delivery. The usual procedure is to prepare a skeleton script with key words or phrases which will allow you to springboard into the actual presentation. An example is given below.

(Slide 7)
    Alternative 2—(repeat structure)
        Expansion—new factory
            —new machines old factory
            —new products (but cut old)
            —go for broke; motivation; excitement

These notes must be carefully laid out so that you will always know precisely where you are. You should also be thoroughly familiar with the link between the key word or phrase and what you actually want to say. There is nothing like the moment of panic that occurs when you read a key word and have no idea why you put it there! Visual aid cues, stage directions and reminders can also be added to your 'script'.

Rehearsal

It is asking for trouble to go into an oral presentation without rehearsing. You should attempt at least one full-scale dress rehearsal. If there is a high assessment mark attached to the presentation you may want to do more. Rehearsal is best in front of a sympathetic audience. A classmate, or failing that a friend, are the most obvious choices. Rehearsing into a tape recorder is a good second best. Rehearsing by oneself is useful but not ideal: it is not easy to provide one's own feedback. Rehearsal should also cover the use of visual aids. Visual aids seem to cause more consternation among novice presenters than any other aspect of presentation. Carrying out physical acts in front of an audience when nervous seems to invite disaster.

Familiarity

One of the keys to good presentation is confidence. This stems largely from the knowledge that you know what you are going to be doing. Rehearsal helps, but it is also important to know your material so well that you can move from one part of a presentation to another without getting confused. The less you have to rely on your notes, the more time you have to concentrate on delivery, assessing audience reaction, and enjoying yourself.

    Finally, it is important to repeat a point made earlier. The quality of an oral presentation, perhaps more than any other kind of presentation, is determined by the quality and quantity of the preparatory work. In my experience, 'It will be all right on the night' is not a good guiding principle.

13.3.2 Oral Presentations—Execution

There are some general rules of speaking which may help you in an oral presentation. But beware; expert communicators break them everyday, but still manage to communicate well. It would be best to treat them as suggestions rather than dogma.

(a) Prepare your stage. Arrive early, make sure you know where everything is and familiarize yourself with the speaking position.

(b) Make an interesting start. Set the tone for your presentation by saying something that grabs the audience's attention (e.g., 'I recommend that we close this company down.').

(c) Speak slowly. Your audience must have time to hear and think about what you say. Speak at the rate that the 'slowest' listener can cope with.

(d) Pause. Allow time for the message to sink in and for you to marshal your thought for the next sentence. Don't be afraid of silence. Use pauses for dramatic effect.

(e) Speak audibly. Sound carries most effectively in straight lines. Look up at the audience, not down into your notes.

(f) Introduce variety. Vary the length of sentences and pauses, the pace of presentation and the pitch of your voice. (Nothing is more boring than a monotone delivery.)

(g) Let the audience read the visual aid. Just because you know what's on it doesn't mean they do. Pause and let them take it all in before expanding on its content.

(h) Use your eyes. Maintaining eye contact with your audience is important. It signals confidence, interest and concern and tells them that the message is important. It also keeps your head up!

(i) Position yourself correctly. Stand centre, in full view with your head up and talk directly to all the audience. Don't stand bent over notes or hide behind the lectern or overhead projector.

(j) Move, but not too much. Complete immobility suggests lack of confidence or interest. Excessive gesticulation conveys nervousness. Movement can be used creatively to suggest interest, excitement and commitment, but don't overdo it.

(k) Think positively. Confidence feeds on itself—it can grow if you believe in yourself and are determined to succeed. If you approach the presentation tentatively and with doubts this will affect your peformance and the audience's perceptions of that performance. Confidence will then disappear and the downward spiral will begin.

13.4 WRITTEN ANALYSES OF CASES

Written analyses of cases (known at Harvard as WACs) are usually used together with case discussions or oral presentations. They may be handed in at the time of the discussion or students may be allowed to include material from the discussion in their written presentation which is handed in at a later date. WACs are frequently required to take a management report format.

13.4.1 Written Analysis of Cases—Preparation

Preparation for writing up a case analysis involves thinking mainly about its structure and its audience. The process will start with your virgin case notes and end with a detailed structural outline.

Audience

The audience for a written presentation is almost always confined to the case instructor. He will provide you with the formal parameters such as length, structure, style, submission date, assessment criteria, etc. However, there are also informal parameters which should govern your preparation. These are largely concerned with the case instructor's own likes and dislikes, preferences and requirements. These may be trivial (an aversion to green ink) or important (a requirement that all benefits and disbenefits should be quantified).

Trivial preferences can be met with a minimum of compromise. If you do not meet them you simply make the message more difficult to understand. However, if you do not share your case instructor's views about the case or how it should be written up then the problem is more difficult. You can choose to capitulate and write what he wants to read. Alternatively you can choose to do it your way. You may, for example, wish to structure your report in a different way to that demanded by the case instructor. You may choose to recommend a course of action that values human freedom over economic advantage knowing that your instructor believes otherwise. What you should do in these situations is to signal the differences where they become most apparent. You have to alert the case instructor to the fact that you may be disagreeing with him. This at least should help him assess your work using criteria of logic, creativity, presentation and so on, rather than those of philosophy or values.

Whether you decide to compromise or confront, two points are vital. The first is to try to understand instructors as human beings rather than totally rational objective people. The second is to make a conscious decision as to which alternative to choose in the light of what you seek to get out of the case course.

Structure

The development of a written document should be essentially a top-down process. First the main headings, then the subheadings and paragraph descriptions and finally the actual writing. A written case analysis is rather like telling a story. A certain amount of character development or scenic description is helpful, even vital, but the story line must be maintained intact throughout if the reader is going to understand. Working from the top downwards ensures that the story line is kept intact. You may not get the structure or content right the first time. You may decide to change the structure while actually writing. This is fine, providing that the whole structure is written out again and not just kept in your head, half-remembered and vague.

There are four decisions concerning structure which have to be made when writing a report. These are structure visibility, headings, sequence and length.

Structure visibility

The two extremes are the essay and the management report. An essay is a uniform piece of writing with no headings or subheadings, maintaining structure by means of a logical thread. By contrast, management reports involve several nested layers of headings, categorizing small blocks of text which may themselves be simply numbered points.

Few case instructors allow students to write case analyses in essay form. On the other hand, there is usually still some choice about the amount of structure you wish to display. The decision should turn upon the type of case analysis you have carried out. If it requires long, interconnected, complex arguments then less structure should show. The flow should be uninterrupted by headings or subheadings. If on the other hand there is a lot of detail and disparate material to communicate then a management report style would be more appropriate. It should also be noted that it is easier to use a highly structured report as the basis for a case discussion since the analyses are neatly catalogued.

It is fairly clear that there is no universal agreement on what a written case report should contain or what order should be used. This is hardly surprising, but it needs demonstrating. There are some cases, for example alternative 5 in table 13.2, where it would be necessary, or even just more interesting, to develop a structure specifically for that case. An example of this might be to write an imaginary letter to the chief executive of the company described in the case. In some instances the case itself will suggest a structure. As always the criterion should be the effectiveness of the communication. If a specific and idiosyncratic structure makes the message clear and interesting, then use it.

Headings and subheadings

Is there one ideal structure for all case study reports, or should the structure depend on the case? An examination of table 13.2 is instructive

1. Summary
       Purpose
       Scope
       Conclusion(s)
       Recommendations
   Introduction
   Body
   Appendices

2. Problem statement
   Factors causing the problem
   The effects of the problem
   Examination of the possible solutions and their implications
   Conclusions
   Recommendations
   Appendices

3. Title page
   Table of contents
   List of exhibits
   Summary of recommendations
   Background material and facts
   Statement of problem
   Analysis
   Solution and implementation
   Appendices

4. Principal message
   Why it was chosen
   Why others not chosen
   Evidence supporting the analysis

5. The situation in the tool room
   What I would do
   Why I wouldn't close down the factory
   Action plans
   The future

Table 13.2 Alternative Written Presentation Structures

in this respect. It compares a number of structures which have been recommended for the reporting of case results.

Sequence
In what order should the sections be placed? The obvious answer to this question is to place them in a logical order which carries a clear story line.

However, there are two major logics which can be used in a report of this kind. The first is a sequential build-up of evidence until the denouement is reached in the final section. This is generally regarded as the academic model. The second is the reverse, starting with a clear statement of the outcomes of the analysis and then filling in the detail in the rest of the report. This is a typical management report sequence. The 'academic' approach is easier to sequence since the logic is so much stronger. However, it is less interesting to read and it is difficult to keep the tension building up until the final section where all is revealed. The 'management' approach is more direct, exciting and punchy, but more difficult to sequence. The academic approach is probably better for complex, analytical cases. The management approach works best for simpler, more action oriented, case situations.

There are other possible components of a case report which can only be described as housekeeping. A clearly set out title page with all the relevant information on it can save the case instructor's time and effort. It also makes a good impression, both on the reader and the writer. For the writer it sets the tone for what will follow and makes him raise his eyes from the task of matching words to ideas towards the more important goal of communication. A contents page is also useful and performs a somewhat similar function. It conveys the structure of the report very quickly and gives an impression of where the emphasis, at least in terms of word volume, lies. It also allows the reader to find his way round the report at the second reading.

These components of a written report are by no means exhaustive or mutually exclusive. They merely represent a bank of ideas from which you can draw. You may in fact change the components as you get down to writing. The important point is that you consciously choose a way of breaking up the text which best expresses what you want to communicate with your primary audience—the case instructor.

Within the overall sequence there is also a finer level of sequencing to decide upon. The content of a report can largely be divided into points and arguments.

Points are self-contained ('one of the problems is cashflow') and may be conveyed in a single sentence. They can, in theory, be introduced in any order. In practice an ordered sequence communicates better than an unordered one. Points may be ordered in terms of importance, relevance, cost, interest, time, etc.

Arguments have structure because they describe the relationship between things. When an argument is being developed the sequence almost decides itself. Consider the following example:

Argument—a recent increase in profitability is a problem, not a measure of success.

'Profitability has improved from 13% to 16% in the last six months. This has been solely due to a reduction in investment in stocks following the stock reduction programme instituted by consultants. Sales have in fact been falling since availability is a key factor in this market. Stocks have fallen proportionately faster in the last few months but this cannot continue indefinitely. In the near future sales will continue to fall and profitability will eventually slump.'

If the same sentences were rearranged the argument would simply make no sense. They have to be in this, or a very similar, order. A chain of logic is forged: sometimes the links are very obvious, sometimes they are not so obvious and extra links, which serve only the purpose of linking, have to be added.

Length

The length of a report is a major determinant of its content. The crucial decisions that have to be made are how many points, topics or arguments should be included and which they should be. The first task is to produce a draft outline. This means working through your rough case analysis notes, picking out points, topics and arguments and noting them down under the appropriate headings. An example might look like this:

        Problems—auditor's report
                        Benson's behaviour, effects of sacking,
                        Chief Accountant's background,
                        current position.
                —stock records
                        discrepancies, methods of recording,
                        workers' attitudes.

At this stage it is probably as well to ignore any length restrictions. The notes should be just explicit enough for you to know what they mean when you reread them. The next step is to make a rough estimate of how many words this draft outline will be converted to when written up. If you really have no idea of the likely relationship it might be worthwhile to write up a short section from the outline. This can then be used to determine a rough conversion factor.

You may believe that you can comfortably fit within the word limit and so proceed to convert the points in the draft outline into prose. More likely you will discover that your report is going to be too long. Editing then becomes the order of the day. Firstly you must be sure that there is no repetition in the outline. Secondly you may be able to condense by moving material to an appendix or by using a graphic presentation. Thirdly you may simply have to cut material, but beware that in this process you do not harm the logic, impact or readability of the report. In particular, leaving out lighter points can make the presentation turgid and difficult to read.

Controlling the overall length of a report is important. Allocating words between sections is not. Topics must be placed logically within one of the section heads that you have decided upon. This may produce sections of varying length but this is no great problem: at least it adds variety to the presentation.

13.4.2 Written Analysis of Cases—Execution

The next stage is the conversion of a detailed structural outline into a finished report. This is achieved by the creation of paragraphs, sentences, graphics and presentation.

Paragraphs

Intelligent use of paragraphs can add enormously to the impact and readability of a report. Most of the time a paragraph should be confined to the discussion of a single topic. It is a useful discipline to name the subjects of a paragraph before you begin writing. With a highly visible structure these names correspond to the sub-headings. In a freer format they will serve to remind you what message the paragraph must convey.

Paragraphs are needed because the reader's attention span is short. However, as well as encapsulation the reader needs continuity. He needs to be motivated to continue and to be shown the relationship between blocks of writing. Links are necessary. Links can be provided by a numbering system ('The fourth reason . . .'), by echoing the last sentence in the previous paragraph or by contrast ('An altogether different aspect . . .'). Missing links can be used to signal the end of a major topic or to add emphasis to a point. Variety is important. Too many linked paragraphs lead to a boring sameness. Too few links make a report episodic and difficult to read.

Sentences

Actually writing the sentences that will be read is the final act in creating a report. There are a number of excellent texts on the writing of English and it would clearly pay to study them. However, there are a number of errors that writers of case analyses are particularly prone to and it is worth briefly pointing out how to avoid these:

(a)   Write simply. Complexity of expression does not imply depth of thought. It often indicates poor communication skills, muddled thinking or a smokescreen to hide a failure to understand.

(b)   Write briefly. Most case reporters persist with long sentences in the mistaken belief that they are more impressive. Occasional long sentences are necessary to convey ideas or to add variety, but the average length should be held down.

(c)   Avoid wordy phrases. For example, 'It is a fact that' or, 'There is no way that' are examples of this genre. They aren't really required: they simply add to your word count and blur the message.

(d)   Reduce qualifications. 'It is possible that' and 'If the present situation continues' are phrases that allow you to hedge your bets. They also make your writing more difficult to understand. Try to reduce qualification to a minimum.

(e)   Avoid evaluative language. Words like optimum, best, worst or even good and bad should be carefully considered before they are used. They imply you are making value judgements. This is fine if you are aware of the value basis for those judgements. Otherwise it is evidence of sloppy thinking or inadequate expression.

(f) Add variety. Written case analyses require that a lot of work be levered into a small space. The process of rewriting and editing usually increases the denseness of the writing. If the result is to be at all readable, a little leavening must be added back. This may be done in terms of structure or language. The effect should be one of creating contrast, interest or amusement.

(g)   Think of the audience. Above all keep in your mind the person for whom you are writing. Ask yourself continually, 'Will he be able to understand what I am saying and will he enjoy it?'. It is so easy to forget and commit yourself to getting your analysis on paper, forgetting why you are doing it.

Graphics

Graphics—diagrams, tables or graphs—can summarize or add impact to written text. You should therefore judge whether points can be summarized better graphically or whether a point can be made with more impact as a graph or table before you decide to include them. You should not simply add them in because you have done them.

Knowing why you are including graphics also helps in their design. Graphs and diagrams are frequently too complex. They do not summarize nor do they have impact. Decide what you are going to say and design the graphic to say it. Tables are frequently thrown into reports in their original crude form. The reader is asked to discover the treasure contained within. Frequently they decline and the point is not taken. Constructing tables that communicate is one of the subjects of a useful book by A. S. C. Ehrenberg on the analysis of data (see the section entitled *Further Reading* at the end of this book for more details).

Too many graphics break up the text and make it difficult to read, so be sparing. Too much variety is as bad as too little. Make sure that the graphic and the relevant text are close together, otherwise the point will be lost.

Presentation

The medium is the message. Illegible, badly spelled and scruffy reports on poor quality paper say something to the reader about the writer and his case analysis. It may be the wrong conclusion, but it is virtually unavoidable. Prepare a rough draft first and then convert it into something presentable, checking spellings and making sure your writing is legible. It is likely to be time well spent.

13.5 CASE EXAMINATIONS

Although case examinations take a number of forms, the most common are the seen examinations. These require students to answer questions in the examination room based upon a case study given out some time previously. Students are normally allowed to take their notes into the examination room but the questions are not known in advance.

13.5.1 Case Examinations—Preparation

There are two kinds of activity involved in preparing for a case examination—predicting questions and organizing your case analysis notes so as to answer them.

Predicting questions

I disagree with examiners who argue that students should not attempt to predict questions because 'they are not taking in the full sweep of the syllabus'. It is the examiner's job to ensure that this occurs by setting appropriate questions. Students should be task-oriented and the task is to obtain good examination marks. Predicting questions, however, doesn't guarantee that this will happen.

Predicting questions can only be effective if the process of question-setting is understood. For example, questions may be set by more than one examiner or the examiner may have changed since the previous year. In general case instructors do not try to deceive students. It is in their interest to make sure that examinees understand the questions. Most will be only too happy to discuss the process by which the case is chosen, the questions are set and the criteria by which answers will be judged. This information provides very good background against which more specific predictions can be made.

More specific data comes from past examination papers, past examinees or past examiners' reports. These data enable you to do two things. First of all they allow you to map out the territory covered and areas of concentration. This should influence you only at the most general level. Just because there was a specific requirement for a cashflow forecast last year doesn't mean that it won't be asked for again this year. There may be, however, a general preponderance of quantitative analysis and this may influence your preparation.

The second function in analysing past data is to discover the kind of question asked. Were they specific or general, theoretical or practical, all of one type or various? Understanding the style of questions helps you to organize the material when preparing for the examination.

Organizing Case Material

A case analysis for an examination may follow the stages suggested earlier in the book. However, it should be broader than that carried out for a case discussion or written case analysis. A comprehensive list of problems should be created. Generate a long list of alternatives and evaluate them all. Develop implementation plans for each alternative, not just the preferred one. In this way you will be prepared to move in any direction, to be ready for any contingency. In addition to this very broad coverage you may wish to do more work in specific areas which you judge are favoured by the question setter. Note that this is in addition to, and not instead of, a complete broad analysis.

Do not attempt to prepare answers to specific questions in the hope that they will come up. The chances are that they will not emerge in the expected form, and that having prepared an answer you will be tempted to use it even if it is off target. Worse still, it is difficult to prepare new answers on the basis of old ones. The material is too strictly ordered and specific, and you will not be able to reorganize it in time.

Instead you should organize your case material so that relevant information can be quickly and effectively found, assembled and structured into an answer to a question. It is also worthwhile to convert your rough notes to something approaching final form. This not only saves time in the examination room but prevents misunderstandings. In effect what you will be doing is creating a modular answer kit.

13.5.2 Case Examinations—Execution

There are a number of pieces of advice which apply to any examination but which are particularly important in case examinations.

(a) Analyse the question. Analysis means to break things up into their parts, in this case words and phrases. Ask yourself what they mean. For example:

'Briefly set out the main reasons why the company is facing liquidation.'

'Briefly' and 'set out' suggest that something less than a full discussion is required. Only the 'main' reasons are required so you should not be tempted to pad the answer out with minor reasons. 'Reasons why' suggests that you should be able to link the causes with the effect—a company facing liquidation. This may seem a rather laboured exercise but it forces you to confront the question.

(b) Answer the question. Examinees, on the whole, do not misread questions by accident. They choose to misread them because they cannot answer the question set. A valiant attempt at an answer, however inadequate, should normally be given more credit than pages of off-the-topic waffle.

(c) Prepare a timetable and stick to it. Allocate the time between questions in proportion to the marks they carry. Plan to use at least half your time preparing the answer, the remainder to actually answering it. Failure to stick to a timetable is the single biggest cause of exam failure. The first few marks on a question are easy to earn; the last few are very difficult. Allow time for checking—gross errors reduce credibility.

(d) Structure your answers. This not only makes them easier and quicker to write, it also makes them easier to understand. Even if the detail is inadequate a well articulated structure indicates to the examiner that you have thought about and have attempted to answer the question.

CHAPTER 14

Getting the Most out of Case Studies

It is generally true that you only draw out from a situation in proportion to what you put in. This is particularly true of learning by the case method. Essentially this is a group learning method and students have a responsibility to make the group experience a good and effective one. In addition I would like to give students some suggestions that might help them to get more out of case studies as individuals.

Group responsibilities

There is nothing more demoralizing for a case group than having a number of its members ill-prepared. It is certainly true that case preparation involves a large work load. It is also true that as the course proceeds it becomes easier to disguise the fact that you have done little preparation. Nevertheless lack of preparation effectively sabotages the group's effectiveness and should be fought against.

Case groups usually comprise a rich mix of skills and abilities. It makes sense to draw on this variety and to use it to its best advantage. It also makes sense to help fellow students who are struggling: their difficulties in one area may be compensated by their strengths in others. A supportive and open case group is not only more effective, it is more enjoyable, which in turn makes it a better learning experience for all involved.

In a similar way it is important to recognize the difficulties inherent in the case instructor's role. Leading a case group requires a wide range of teaching skills which few case instructors have in full measure. Try to put yourself in your case instructor's place. Support his positive assets and tolerate his liabilities: intolerance or confrontation can only lead to an unsatisfactory learning experience.

Case studies are only simulations of the real world. Yet they really only become capable of affecting behaviour if you suspend belief and treat them as the real thing. Try to throw yourself into the case situation and accept the occasional absurdities. Case studies allow you to explore feelings and emotions as well as thoughts and ideas.

Because case studies move into real world situations they can raise ethical issues which more prosaic learning experiences do not. In particular you must be careful to treat your fellow students' values with respect, even though they may be cloaked in the proposed solution to a particular problem. Cases allow individuals to explore ideas, roles, feelings, etc. Such explorations should be rewarded rather than punished. In some situations moral judgements may have to prevail over rational ones. In a similar way you have a responsibility to the organization upon which the case is based. They are unlikely to cooperate a second time if hoards of students descend upon them with a view to abstracting further information: they have earned their right to privacy.

Individual Development
Really getting involved in a case—whether it is a case discussion or an oral presentation—brings its own rewards. You have the chance of developing your skills and abilities by practice rather than by cerebration. You may occasionally make a mistake and look silly, but this is a small price to pay for accelerated individual development.

One of the themes of this book has been that case analysis, normally conducted, is a social process. As such it deserves as much attention as the content of the case. It is a great mistake to ignore this obvious point: it not only means a lost opportunity but it also constitutes a threat to effective case analysis. If you cannot learn from the real life behaviour of the case group, how can you expect to learn from the dead world of the written case material.

Feedback has been mentioned before as a key element in learning, but it deserves emphasizing again. If you wish to learn you must get feedback on your performance. The greater the quantity and variety of feedback, the better, all things being equal. It is not easy to obtain nor is it always easy to accept, but it is a very valuable commodity.

Too few students create a permanent record of the more cognitive aspects of case analysis. It is very valuable to take notes in case discussions or presentations. You may pick up interesting facts, ideas, concepts and principles which are worth remembering and even following up. Perhaps more importantly you may wish to record insights about how you or the group have behaved. In any case you should make your notes as soon after the session as possible. It is easy to put off the task and thereby forget it.

I hope that by reading this book you will have been made aware of the options open to you. In turn, therefore, you should be making conscious choices with regard to case analysis rather than being unaware of the variety of choices open to you. I hope you aspire to move beyond this stage towards developing an approach or style which, though it may draw on the procedures described here, will nevertheless be your own.

Finally, I would like to end on an upbeat. The case method is potentially one of the most exciting and interesting learning experiences available. Work hard at it when you have to; relax and enjoy it the rest of the time.

Further Reading

Towl, A. R. (1969), *To Study Administration by Cases*, Boston, Division of Research, Harvard University Graduate School of Business.
A report on a continuing investigation of the case method as practised at Harvard. Lots of very useful peripheral material but mainly for case instructors.

Ronstadt, R. (1977), *The Art of Case Analysis: A Student Guide*, Needham, Mass., Lord Publishing Company.
Should be subtitled 'How to survive a Harvard Case Course'. Down to earth but deals with the detail of case analysis rather than the substance. Includes a worked case analysis example.

O'Dell, W. F., Ruppel, A. C., and Trent, R. H. (1979), *Marketing Decision Making: Analytical Framework and Cases*, Cincinatti, Ohio, Southwestern Publishing Co.
Not specifically about case analysis but uses cases to illustrate a general problem solving approach. Useful and interesting, if a little too general for case preparation.

Tagiuri, R. (1968), *Behavioural Science Concepts in Case Analysis*, Cambridge, Mass., Harvard.
A rather specialized book which provides examples of using theoretical concepts and frameworks in order to analyse case studies. Worth reading if you find application of theory to case material difficult.

McNair, M. P. (1954), *The Case Method at Harvard Business School*, New York, McGraw–Hill.
Rather dated collection of papers about the case method generally but it does include a number of worked case analyses and commentaries which might prove useful.

Reynolds, J. I. (1980), *Case Method in Management Development*, Geneva, International Labour Office.
This book covers case analysis, case teaching and case writing as well as a number of organizational cases. The first section—around 30 pages—presents a very condensed approach to case analysis which is similar to the one outlined in this book.

The Case Clearing House at Cranfield publishes a number of papers and articles on the case method of which the following are particularly useful.

Hatcher, J., Veghefi, R. and Arthur, W. J. (1973), *The Case Method: Its Philosophy and Educational Concept*, University of North Florida, p. 25.

Handspicker, M. B. (1975), *How to Study a Case*, Case Study Institute, p. 2.

Pamental, G. L. (1978), *Approach to Case Analysis*, Merrimack College, p. 9.

Simmonds, D. D. (1974), *Notes on the Case Study*, Cranfield.

In addition, books of case studies very often devote a few pages to case analysis guidelines.

Other useful books include:

Ehrenberg, A. S. C. (1975), *Data Reduction*, New York, Wiley.
This describes a particularly useful method of analysing the kind of data met with in case studies.

Rickards, T. (1974), *Problem Solving Through Creative Analysis*, Aldershot, Gower Press.
Use this book if you find you are stuck for creative ideas. Catalogues and describes very well a multitude of creativity techniques.

Bird, P. (1979), *Understanding Company Accounts*, London, Pitman.
Any good book on finding your way around company accounts will have a section on financial ratio analysis. This one is particularly good.

Jay, A. (1970), *Effective Presentation*, London, Management Publications Ltd.
A nicely presented (as one might expect) book about all sorts of business presentation including writing reports and making oral presentations.

Little, P. (1971), *Communication in Business*, Harlow, Longman.
Somewhat more basic approach to the subject, it provides the kind of detail that experts often take for granted.

Index